HOW TO DRAW
FACES

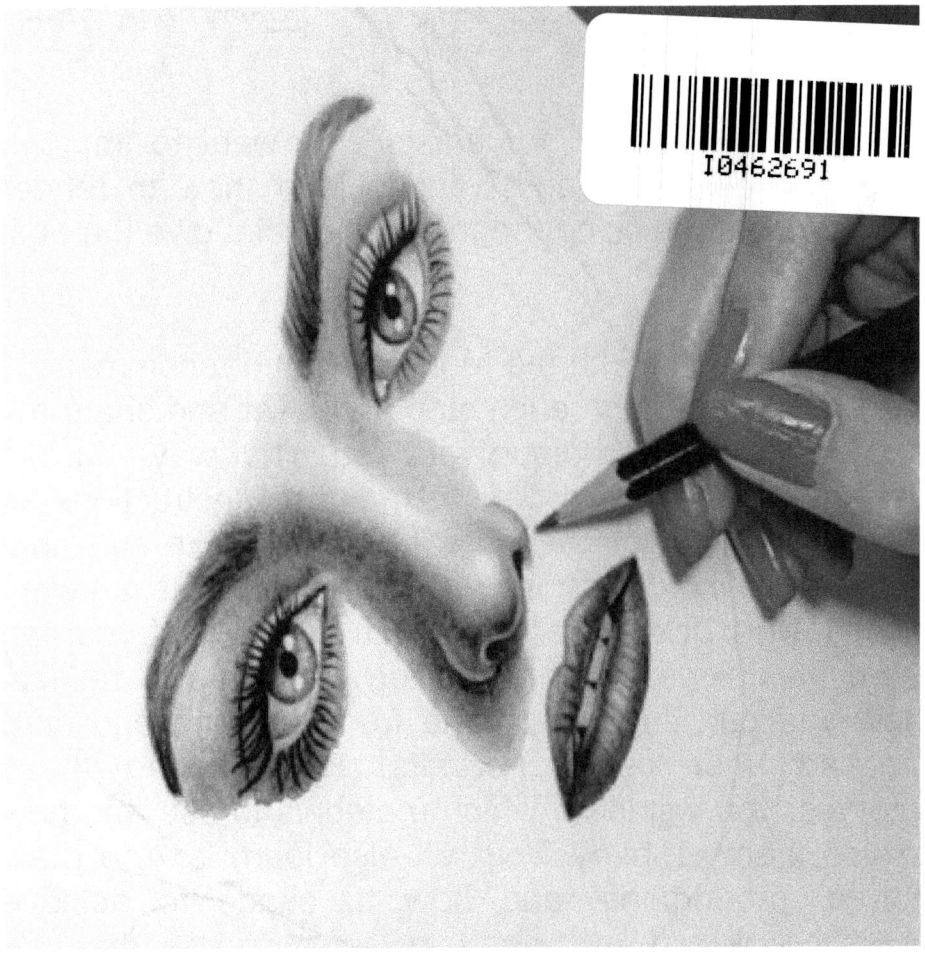

Learn to Draw People from Complete Scratch

by Jasmina Susak

FOREWORD

I created this tutorial for artists who want to improve their drawing skills, and want to learn how to render realistic portraits using the techniques that give the best possible results.

After the chapter with the tools I use and recommend, I will walk you through each step and layer and share my experience and technique with you. That way you can get better results. I've tried to make my instructions as detailed as possible because I want to make sure that you can easily understand what I want to explain. I want to share my drawing process with you so that you can learn the things that have taken me years to realize. Now you can save your time from studying and start creating your pencil portraits. By following these tutorials, you will learn which materials to use and how to use them properly. You will also learn how to draw correct proportions, and how to shade to achieve realistic look.

In this tutorial, you will learn:

How to sketch from complete scratch without using any reference photos

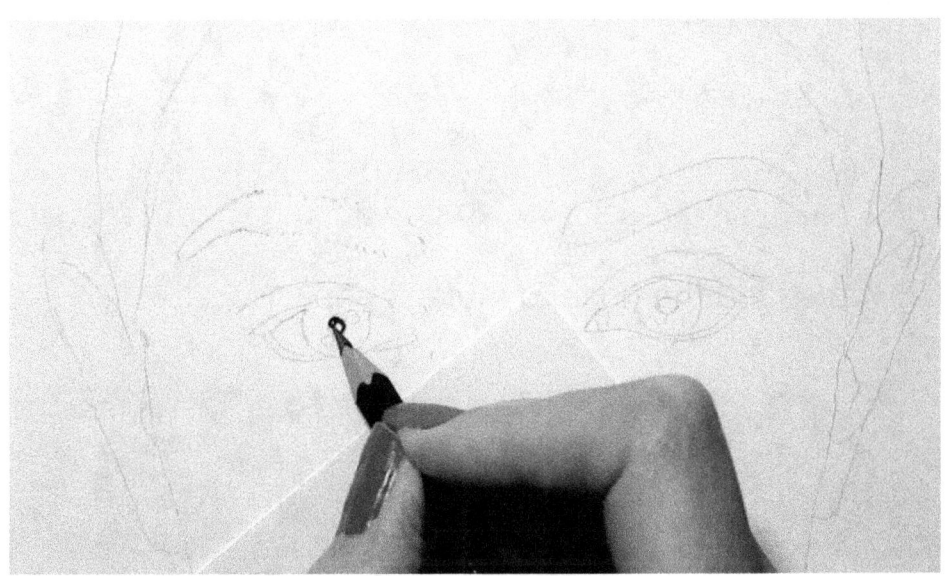

How to draw lifelike eyes and beautiful eyebrows

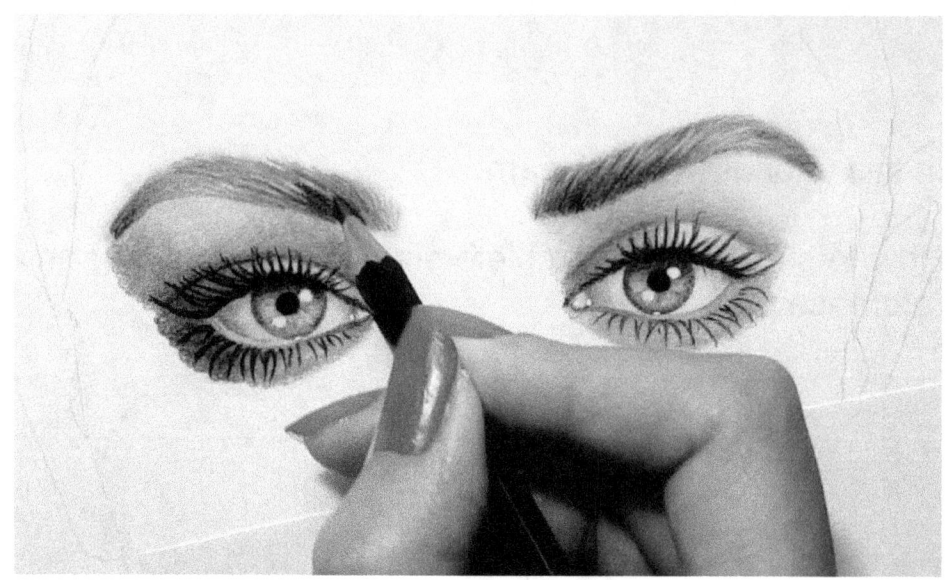

How to shade the nose to make it pop

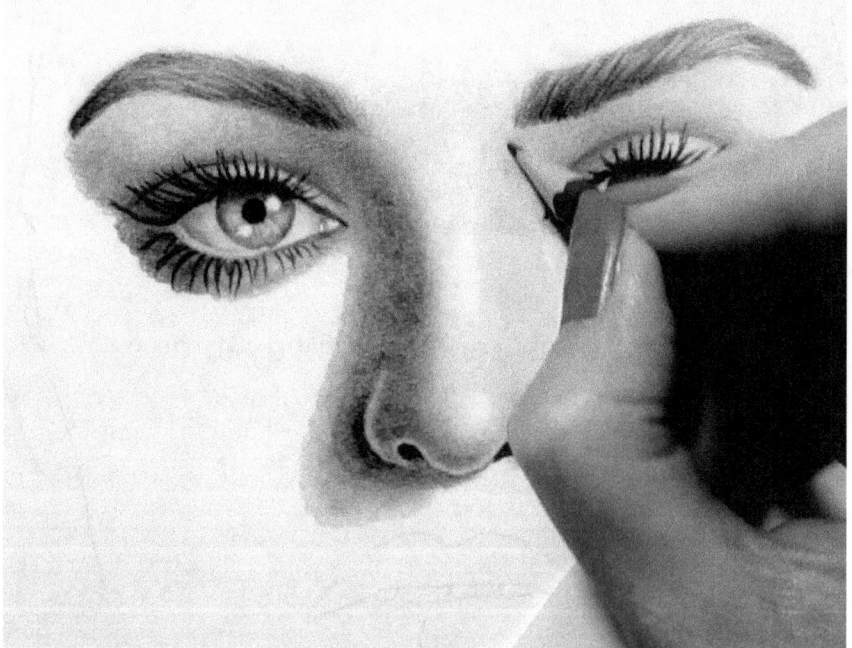

How to draw plump lips and teeth.

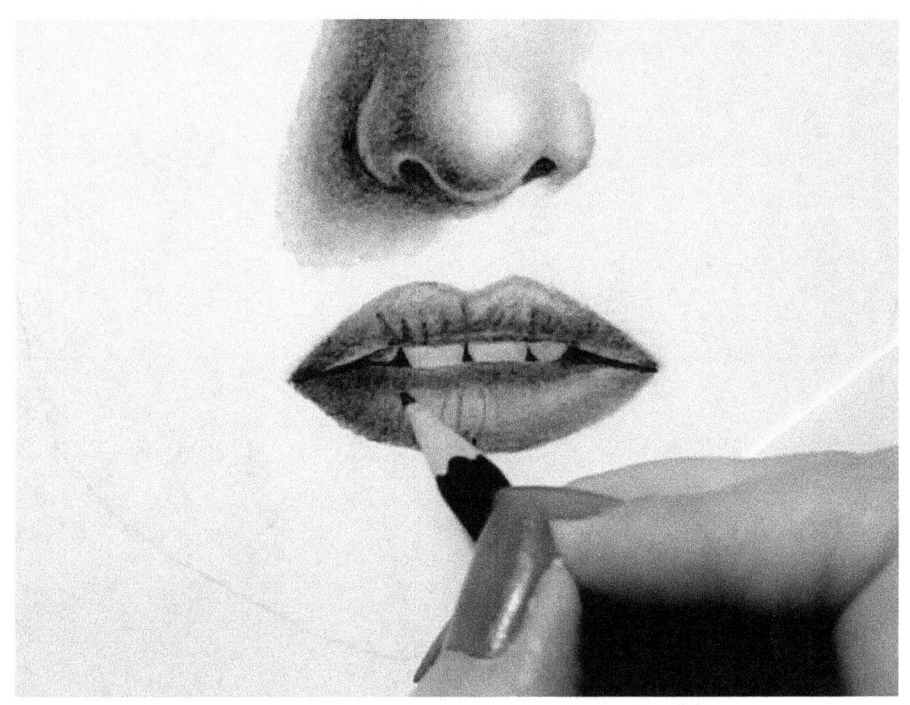

How to patiently shade the skin to make it smooth and achieve the best results

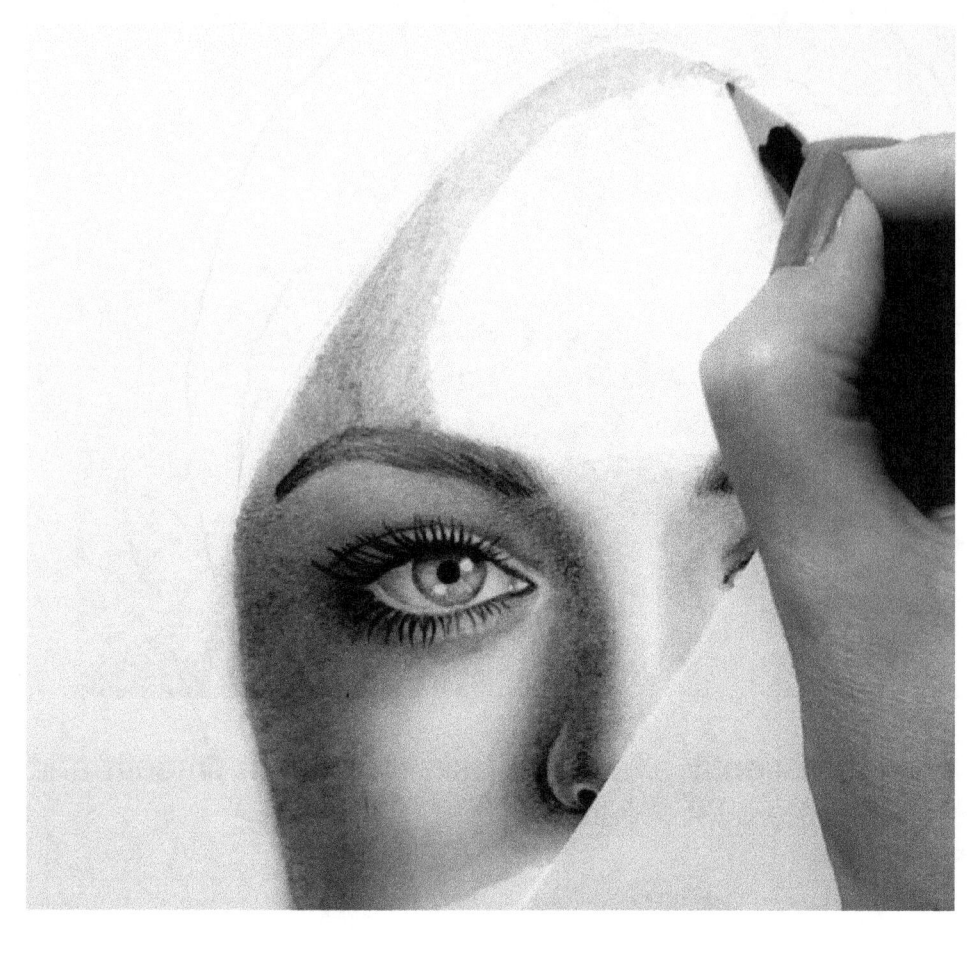

And how to draw realistic hair.

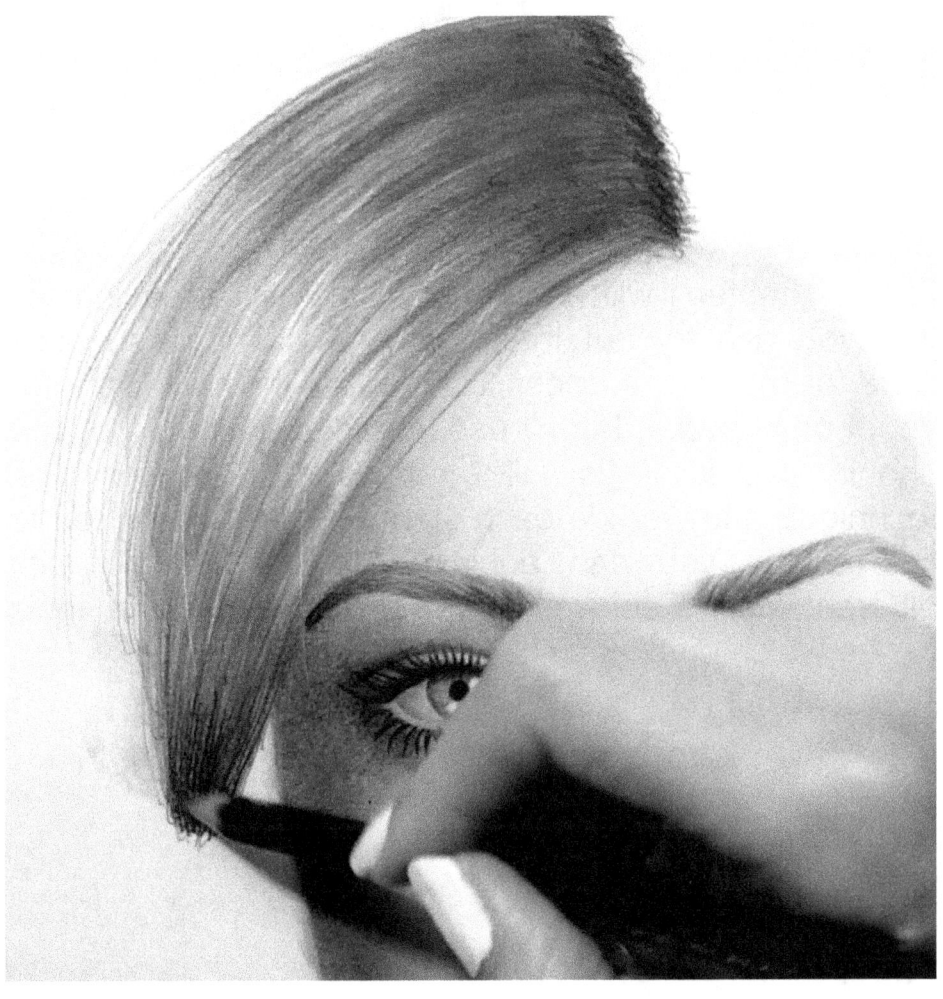

If you are ready for these tutorials, let's get started with materials!

TOOLS

In this chapter I will show you what I will be using, so that you can try out these materials. These supplies work for me, which doesn't mean that they will work for you. For example, I don't use kneaded erasers, but you should use it, if you like this kind of eraser. The technique and work in each step is important for you to follow, and you can achieve the same thing with different tools. Feel free to experiment with other tools to see which ones you like more.

My Art Materials

Paper

For this drawing, I will be using Fabriano Bristol, A4 paper format. I use this paper for both colored and graphite pencil drawings. This paper is very thick, smooth, bright and very heavy. It weights 250 grams per m2, or 145 lbs. So, it's a very good, thick, and durable paper. It's the only paper I use for my drawings.

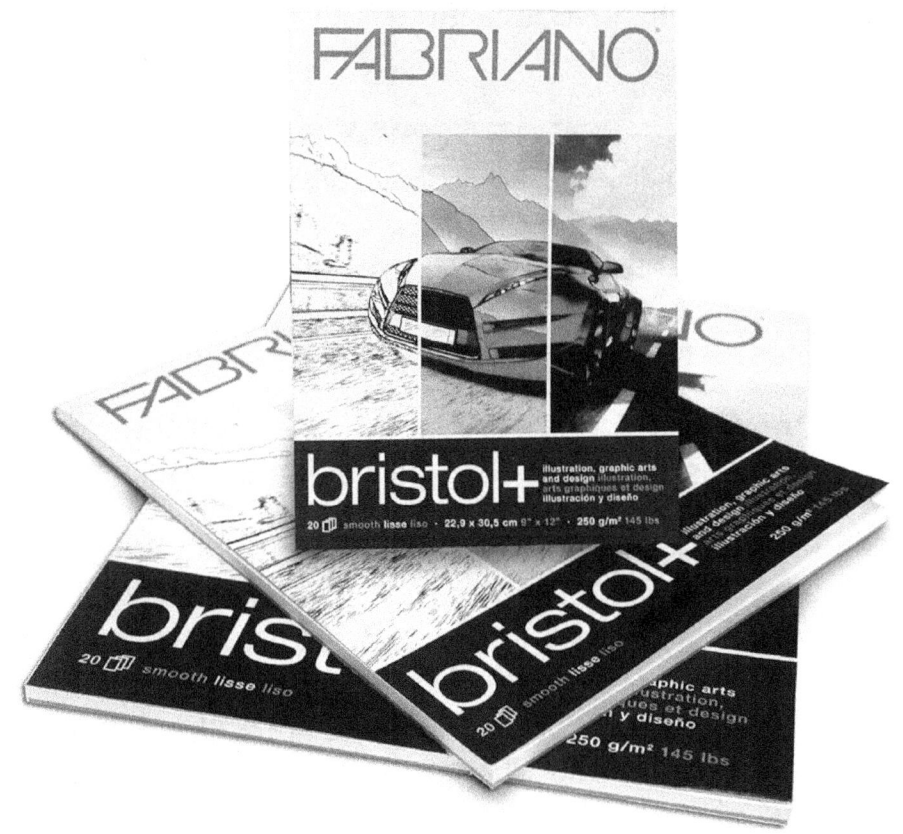

Pencils

I recommend purchasing high-quality graphite pencils, such as Castell 9000 by Faber-Castell that I use, or any other similar brand. For example: Staedtler Mars Lumograph, Derwent Graphic, Prismacolor Premier Graphite Drawing Pencils, Caran D'ache Graphite Line, Faber-Castell Pitt, Koh-I-Noor Hardtmooth, and Lyra Rembrandt Art Design.

In the next image, you can see the nuances of the

pencils that you have available, but you won't need all of them.

9H 8H 7H 6H 5H 4H 3H 2H H F HB B 2B 3B 4B 5B 6B 7B 8B 9B

Hardest   →   Medium   →   Softest

I really just have 5 pencils.

- One 8B, which is very dark. I use it for the for very dark, black areas, such as pupil and similar.

- I have a B, which is still pretty dark, but not as dark as 4B or darker. You can even use a 2B, which is very similar to a B. As you can see they are next to each other on this scale, so there's no big difference. Also, there's no big difference between 4B and 9B, so it's enough if you just get one of these. I have 8B, but you can have 6B or 7B for the parts that I will be using 8B. It is important to have one darker than a B.

- For me, the most important is an HB. With this pencil you can replace nuances from 3H to 2B by changing the pressure.

- A 2H is very good for creating a realistic skin using circular motions.

- I have one 6H which is also very good for brighter areas of the skin and you will see how I will be using it.

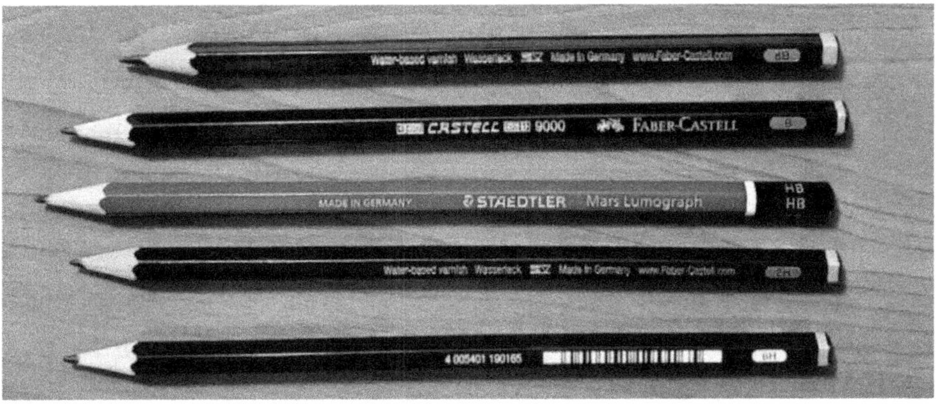

Besides these pencils, I have a simple brandless mechanical pencil. I will be using this for the hair. I use 2B and HB leads for this pencil. This tool is very good for the hair because you can always create the same thickness of the hairs, you don't have to sharpen it. I wouldn't recommend it for the skin. For the skin we need a very dull tip. I will elaborate further when we get to that step.

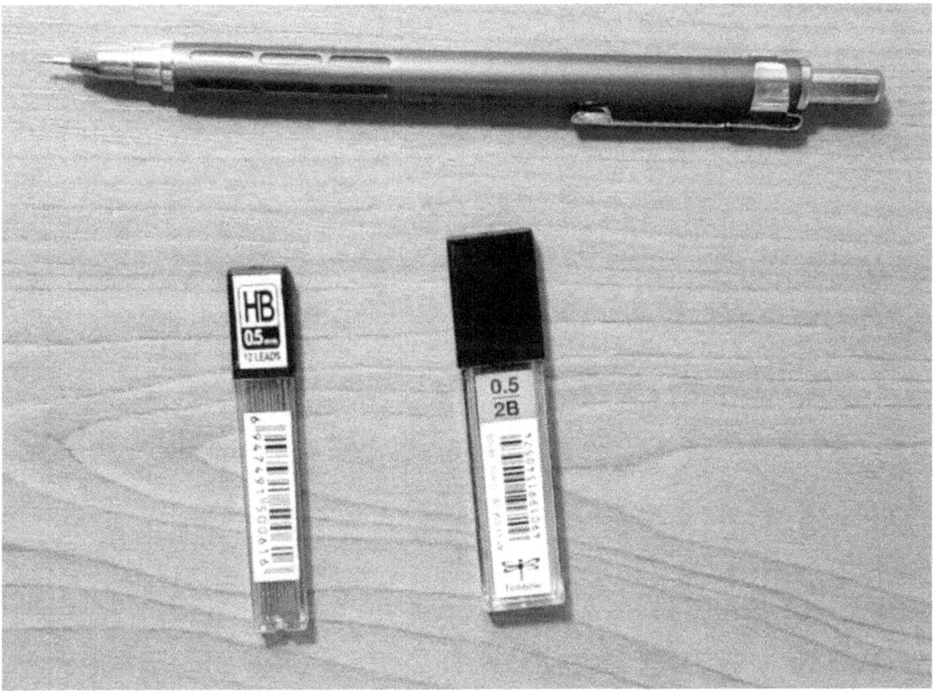

You have to have something for blending the drawn areas. I have these blending stumps in three sizes. This tool is very cheap. You can blend tiny areas with it. I don't recommend this for blending larger areas like the skin. For the skin, we're going to use a paper tissue. You can use the tissue you already have at home, but cotton pads are also good. You can even use toilet paper or kitchen paper towel, it doesn't matter as long as it is not wet and doesn't have any odor.

Also, Q-tips are very important for blending smaller areas, such as the sides of the nose, which is not that small for a blending stump. Throughout these tutorials, I will always mention which tools I will be using, and I will always explain why.

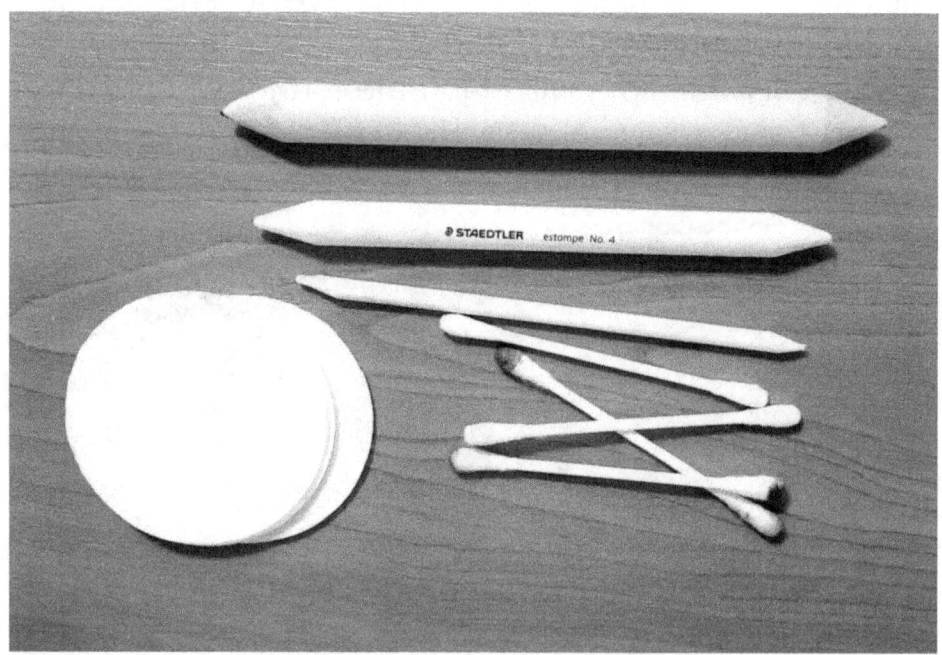

Erasers are very important, but I actually don't use that well-liked kneaded eraser. I use a simple, plastic eraser. I have one eraser in pencil by Faber-Castell, which has red gum on one side, and white gum on the other side. I also have a mechanical eraser by Tombow, which allows me to create very tiny highlights. It has a refillable, round gum and is very practical. It costs about $5 and you can use it for a long time.

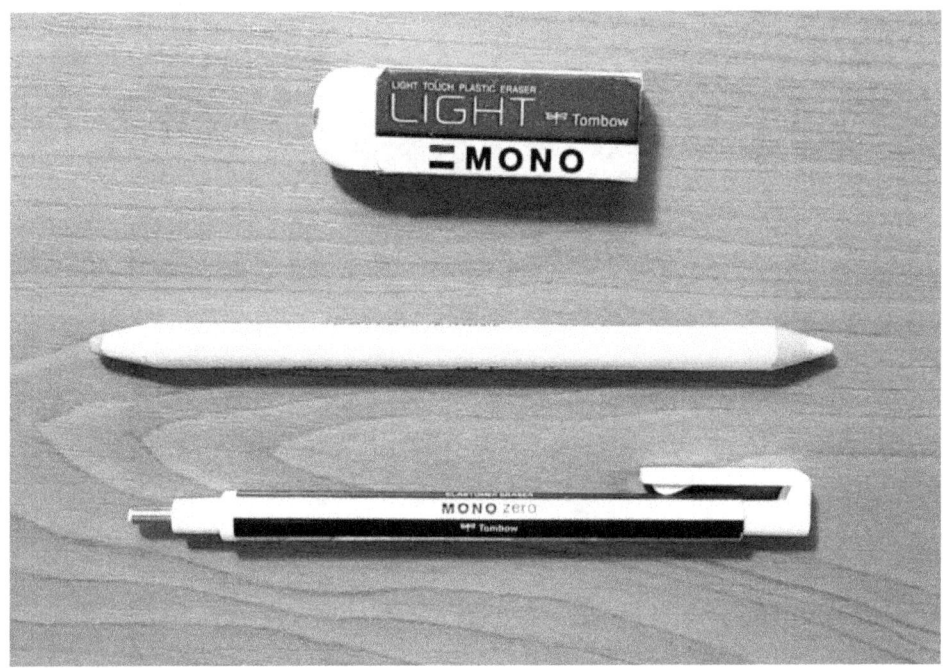

When you can't create very bright highlights by erasing, I recommend purchasing a white ink gel pen or a fine white marker by Uni Posca. These are opaque and you can apply them over the graphite, for example to create the shiny part of the eyes, which will suggest wetness on the eye. You can also highlight hairs and anything you want. I use these for my colored pencil drawings too.

A white ink gel pen costs about $2, and a white marker by Uni Posca about $3-$4. Depending on how often you use them they can last for months.

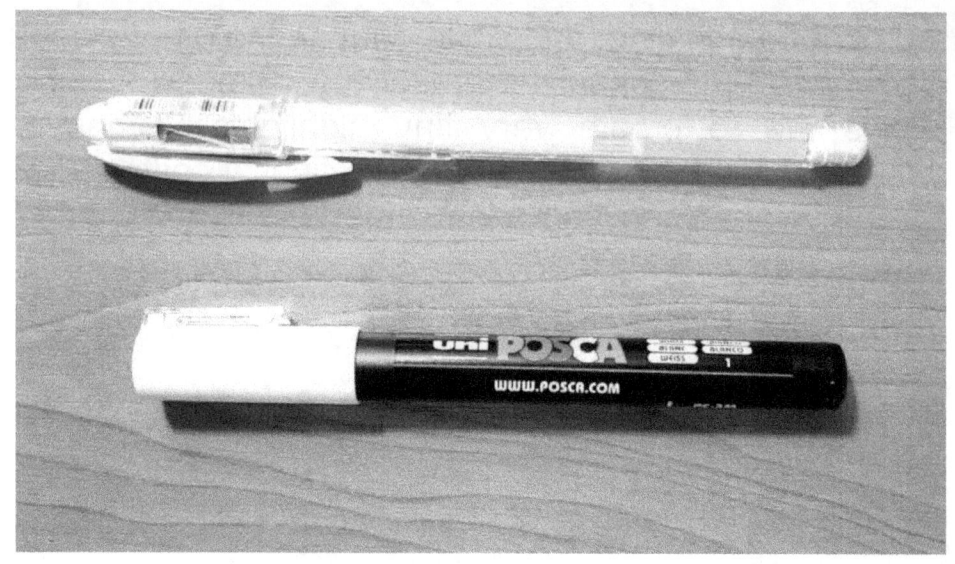

And you will also need a ruler for measuring while sketching.

SKETCHING

The first thing to do is to decide how big you want the face that you draw, and to decide where you want to place it on your sheet of paper.

I want the top of my head about two centimeters, almost 1 inch from the top, where I have drawn one horizontal line. I named it the A line. Then, you need to draw one more horizontal line to determine the position of the bottom of the chin. I named it the B line.

A

B

The next thing is to draw the horizontal line exactly in the middle. To do that, measure between the A and B lines; it's 19,5 centimeters in my case (about 7,5 inches), which means that I have to mark 9 centimeters and 7 millimeters from the top. Do the same on the left and the right sides. When you connect these two marked points you will have the C line.

The pupils will be placed exactly over this C line. Now we already know where to draw the eyes.

Next, you have to determine the width of the face. Take the measure that you took between the A and C lines, in my case it's about 9 centimeters and 7 millimeters, almost 4 inches. Add just 1/3 of that to this measure, to 9,7 centimeters, and you will get about 12 centimeters or 4 3/4 inches. Now, mark this measure of 12 centimeters somewhere in the middle of this C line, and just draw 2 vertical lines. These lines don't have to be strictly parallel to the edge of the paper and to each other, let's name them D lines.

Once we have the frame as guidance, we know where the pupils will be placed.

It's time to draw the outline of the head.

Start at the top, going over the horizontal A line a bit, a few centimeters, then start curving the line downwards. I suggest making dashed lines first, to see whether they will connect with the point between lines D and C. Keep in mind, this outline is not too important because we are going to draw hair over this, but we still need some sketch to serve as a guideline. So, this line is not the outline for the hair cut, but for the skull.

Next you can move to the lower half of the frame. Start on the ends of your outline over the C line, and go downwards, creating a slightly curved line. Here you can make a variety of lines since there are a lot of shapes of the chin. Also, you may draw dashed lines first. I want to draw female, and females tend to have a more refined jawline as well as a more narrow chin. If you want to draw a male, you can create a wider chin. At the bottom of the chin, also follow the B line a bit horizontally, and then start curving it upwards creating some dashed line to see where it will end. So, the shape of the chin can be whatever shape you want. You can't fail here. It can be hard shaped, prolonged, oval, heart shaped, but what I have drawn is one of the most common shapes of the females. You shouldn't make everything symmetric; some imperfections will make your drawing look more natural because faces are not symmetrical, so just try to avoid that.

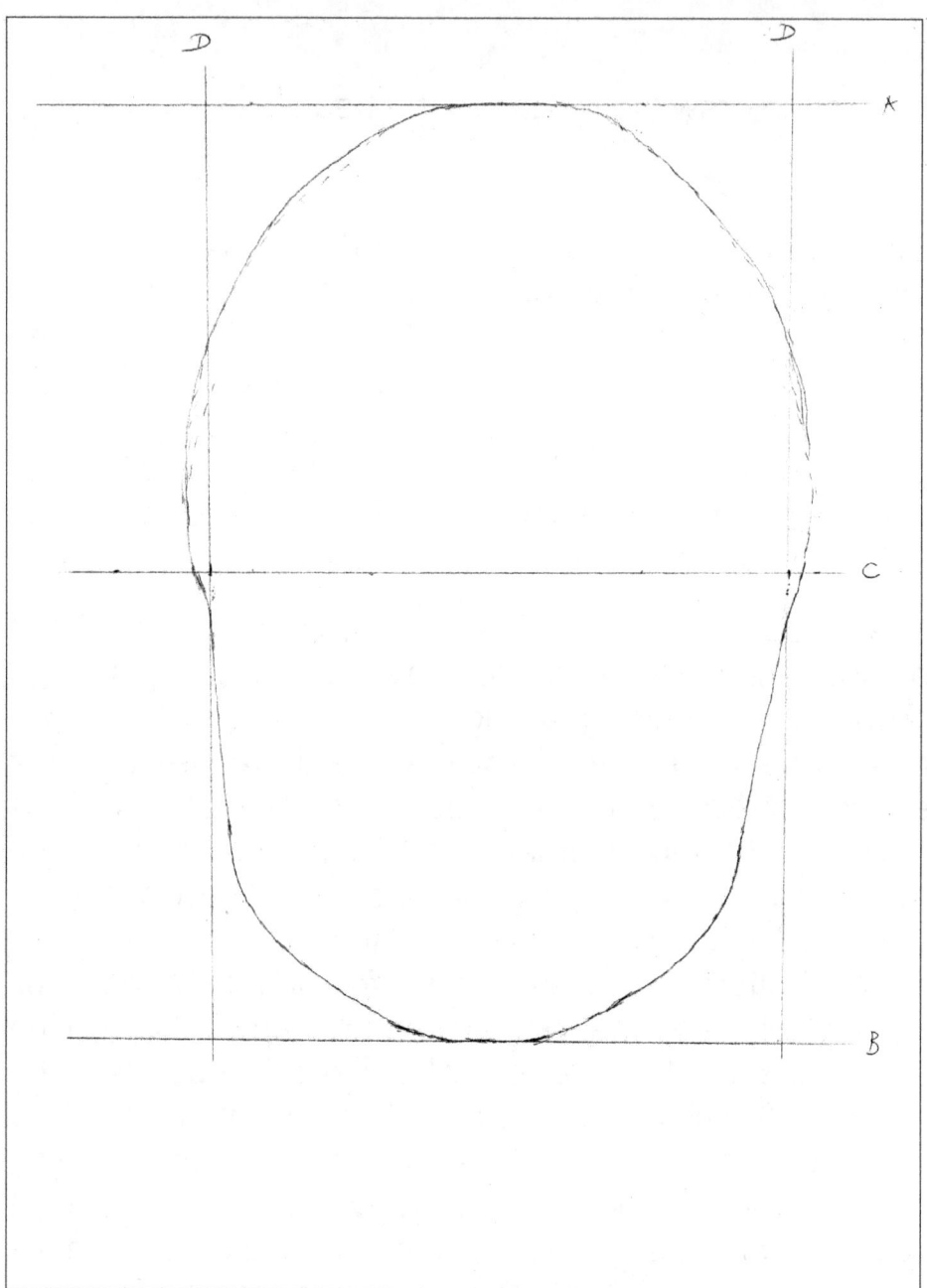

As a next step, let's draw the line between the hair and the skin of the forehead (though it may be drawn anywhere). There are small and big foreheads, so you can't actually draw it incorrectly. I have drawn my outline on 2 centimeters from the top of the head, of the A line.

As you did when outlining the head, you can do the same here. Draw a bit horizontally, and then start to curve the line and draw it towards the cross point between lines D and C, as shown in the next image.

It doesn't have to be perfect, but we need this line for measuring the position of the facial features in the following steps.

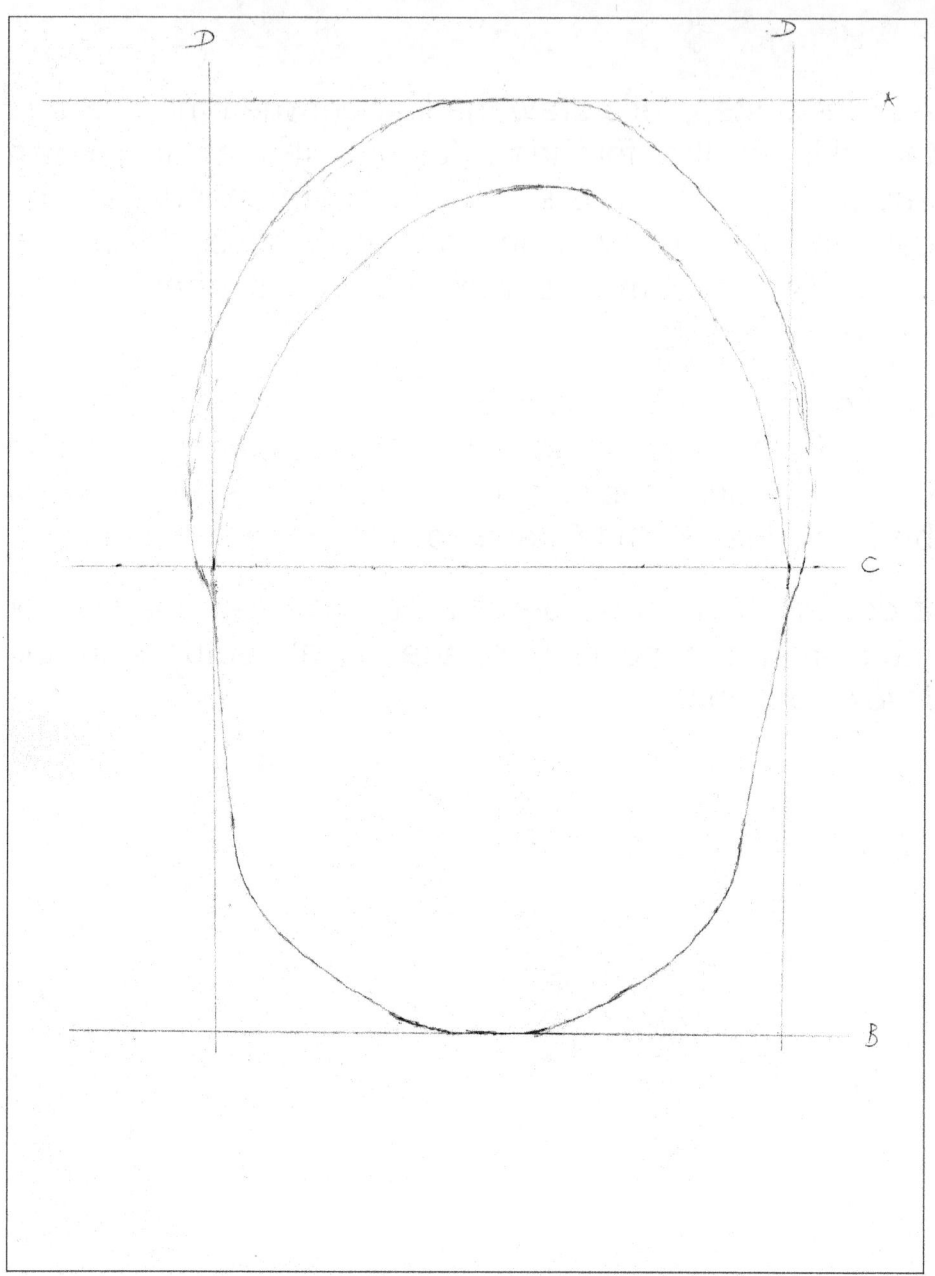

The next thing to do, is to divide this horizontal height of the face, starting from the top of the forehead (not head) to the bottom of the chin, into three equal parts. I have 17.5 centimeters height, so I have to measure from the top between the hair and the forehead quite above 5.8 cm. You can measure in inches, just divide the height that you get by 3. I have named the dashed line on the top of the forehead as M1.

So, from the M1 line to the next, M2 line is 5.8 cm distance. This dashed M2 line is found right above the eyebrows.

Use the same measure to determine the position of the M3 dashed line, which is found right under the bottom of the nose and ears.

The last, M4 line is B line at the same time.

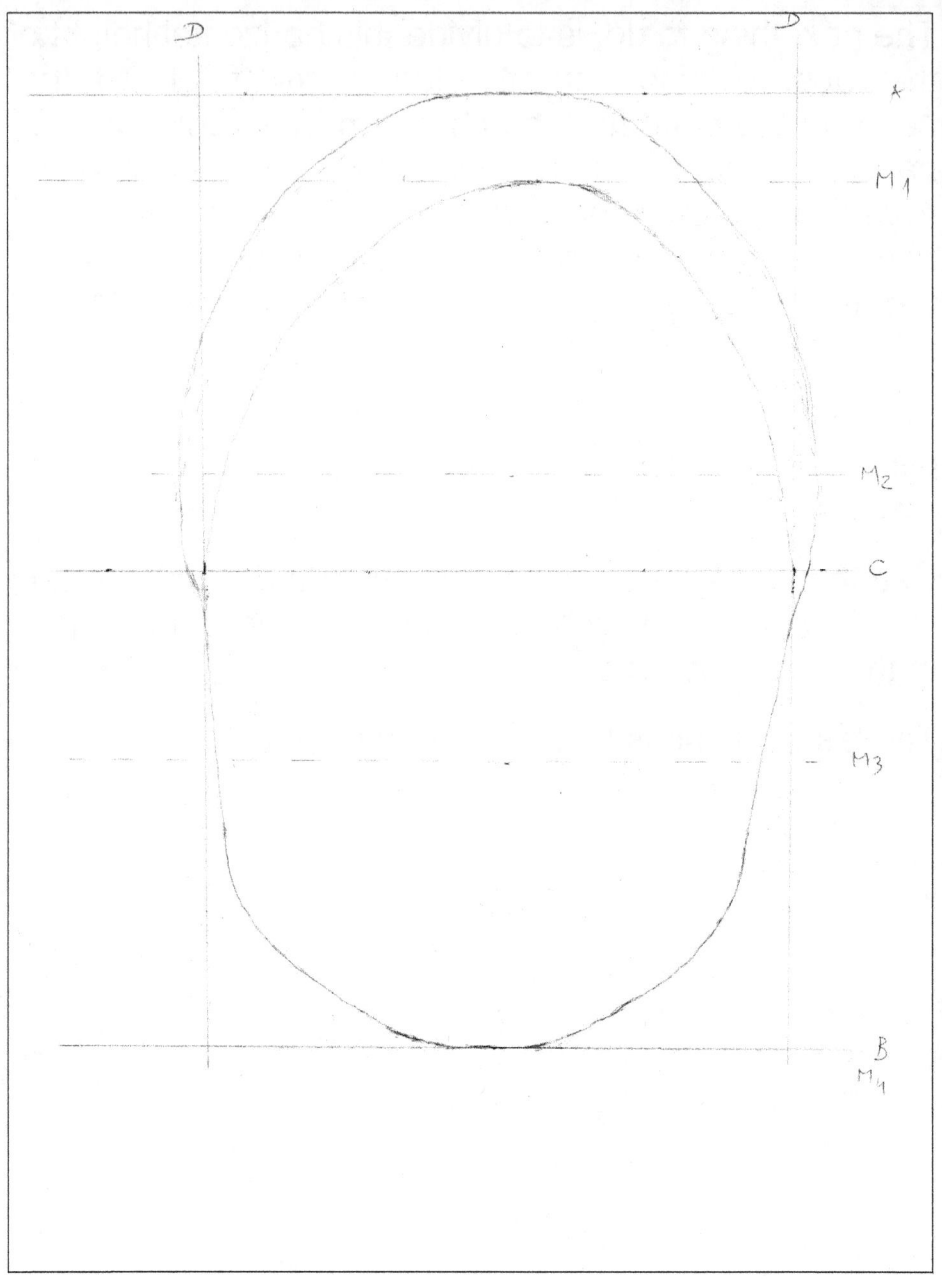

Now we can draw the ears. Top line of the ears is M2 and bottom line is M3, so you have to draw the ears in this space. Of course, it's not in every case the same, so you can draw bigger or smaller ears; closer or further from the face.

The top of the ear can also be of any shape, just draw it a bit further from the face than the lower area of the ear which should be drawn closer to the face.

I will draw the hair over the ears, but I just want to show you where you have to place it if you want to draw, and I will also show you how to shade it.

So, draw a curvy line right under the M2 line, and start curving it downwards. This long line can be parallel to the face outline. Then just curve it towards the face right over the M3 line. Add some details inside this area as shown in the next image.

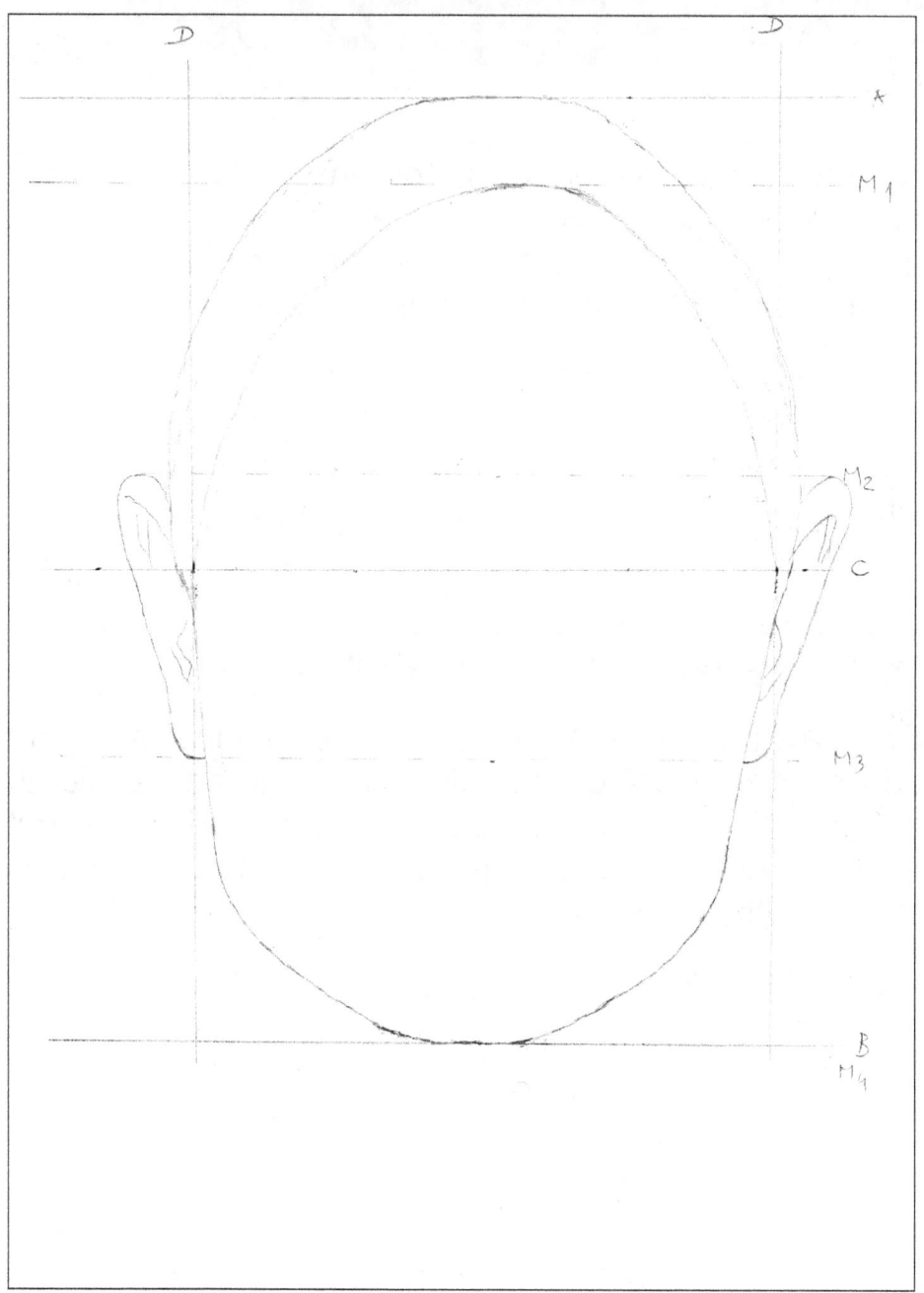

D   D   A

                                                        M₁

                                                        M₂

                                                        C

                                                        M₃

                                                        B
                                                        M₄

To determine the position of the eyes, we have to divide the C line into 5 equal parts, and we have to measure the ears too.

My C line is about 15 centimeters long, so I have made one area 3 centimeters wide. Of course, it doesn't have to be exactly 3 cm, but approximately. I have drawn vertical, dashed lines to divide these areas, to show you where to draw the eyes.

You can draw these lines over the paper because you will have to trace these outlines on a clean piece of paper, anyway. The paper you are sketching now, will become dirty and damaged by erasing.

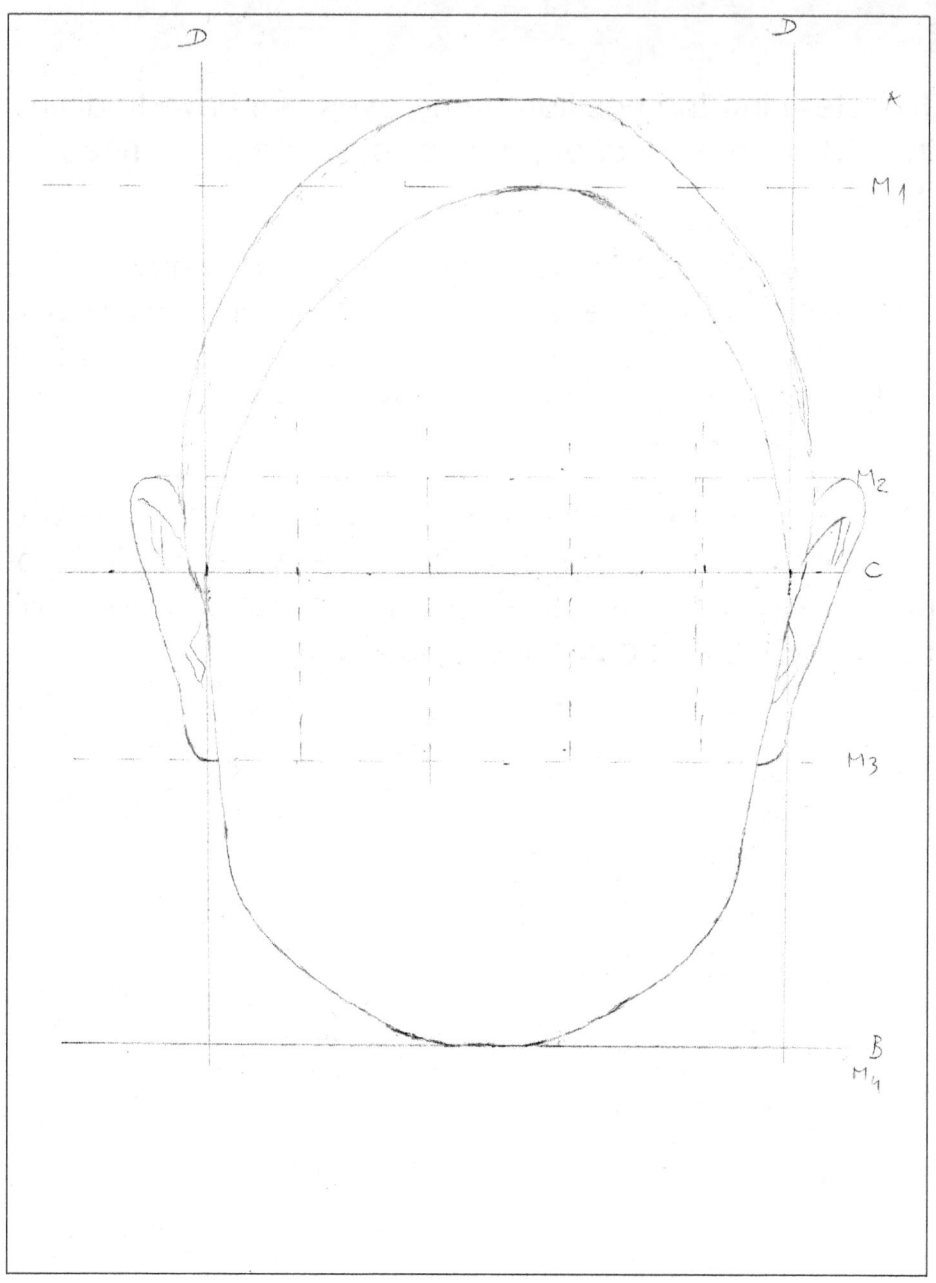

Now that we have these 5 equal areas, let's start with the pupils in the second and fourth areas over the C line. Draw tiny circles for pupils, and draw irises around them. You don't have to draw the upper area of the iris boundaries, but cover it with the upper eyelids.

The width of the eye should fit between two vertical dashed lines, in the second and fourth areas, counting from the left.

The outer corners should be placed right over the C line, but inner corners should be placed a bit under the C line. Study the next image before you draw your outlines. Draw the lower eyelids right under the irises, and make this line less curvy than the line of the upper eyelid. The shape of the eye can also be different. Allso draw the crease, a line above the upper eyelid, parallel to it.

Create a light reflection wherever you want over the iris or pupil. I have marked two: one in the upper-right area of the iris, and one in the lower-left area of the iris. Wherever you draw these light reflections, make sure to draw the same on both eyes. Also, mark the tear duct in the inner corners of the eyes. So, actually between two eyes we should have the width of an eye, so that's an important rule to keep in mind when drawing portraits. As always, there are exceptions where the distance can be a bit smaller or larger.

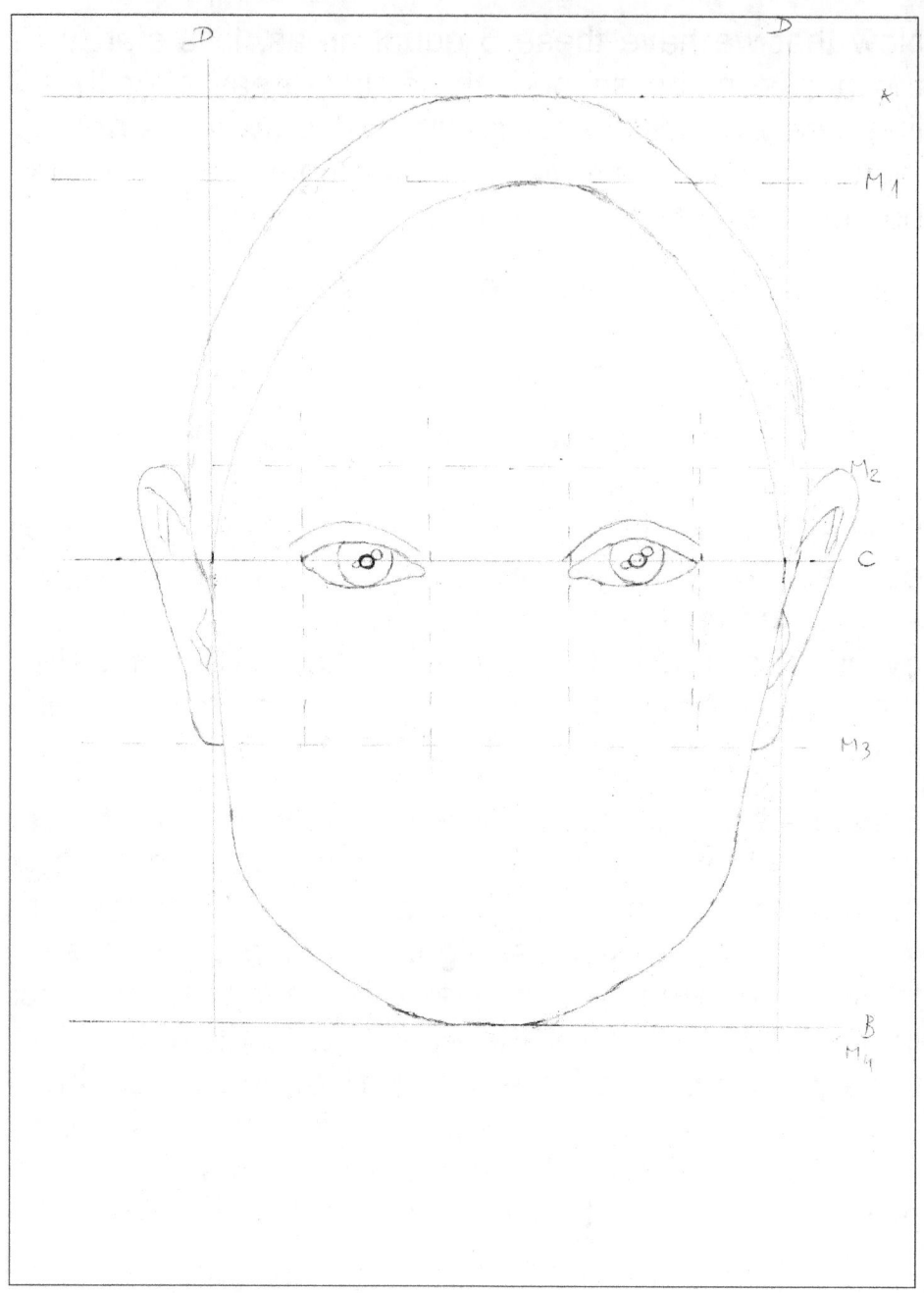

The M2 line is usually found right above the eyebrows, so it can help you determine the position of the eyebrows. I wanted to draw female eyebrows that are a bit more arched on the highlighted part of the bottom area of the forehead, next to the temple. So for that side, in my case, will go a bit over the M2 line.

If you draw a male portrait, draw them right under the M2 line.

Your eyebrows don't have to be of the same shape as mine; there are a variety of shapes and sizes that can be chosen instead of these. Try to make them the same, yet not absolutely symmetrical. The eyebrows are usually thicker next to the nose, and thinner next to the temple, so you should think about this when outlining the eyebrows.

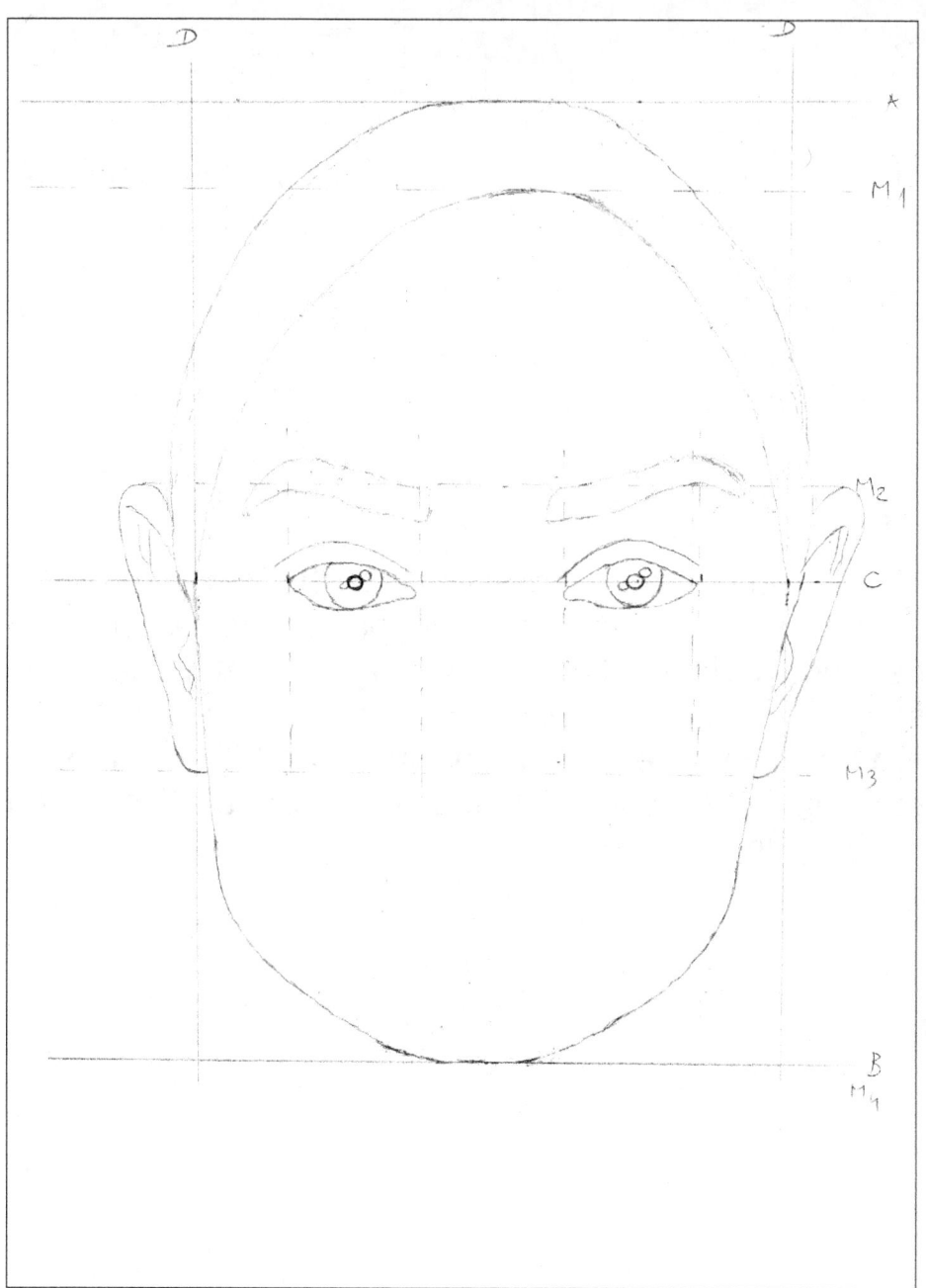

The bottom of the nose should be placed right under the M3 line, but the top can reach a little bit under this line.

The rims of the nostrils shall be placed right under the tear duct, to fit in the mid area of those 5 equal parts that we divided with vertical dashed lines. These 2 dashed lines can help you to place the nose within this area.

Outline the nostrils too, and since the nose contains shades mostly, we just have to determine the position of the nostrils, rims, and the bottom of the nose.

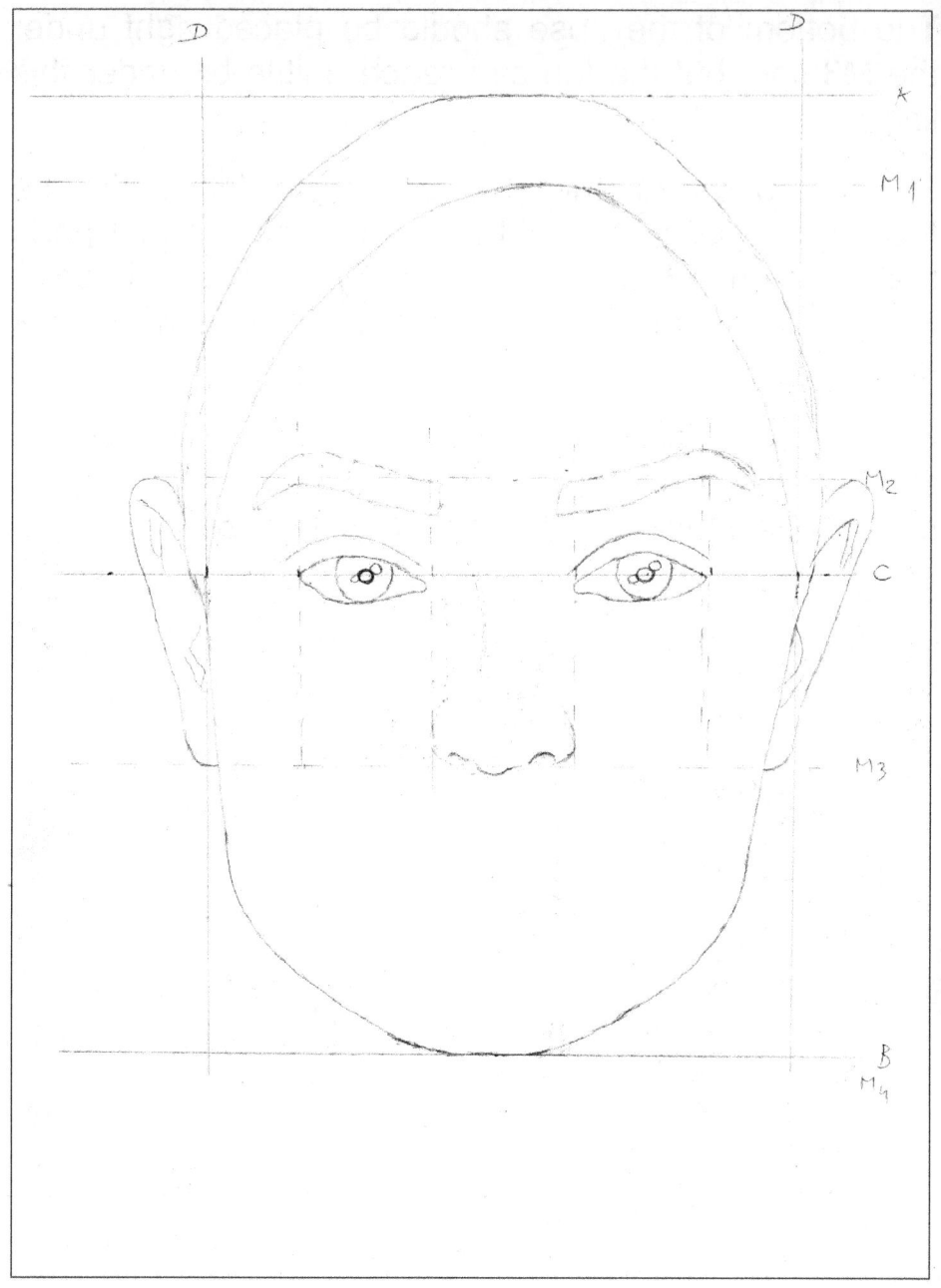

Lastly, determine the position of the lips. The corners of the lips should be placed under the pupils or the inner iris boundary, I mean in the same vertical line.

You can create any shape of the lips, so anything can work. There are many kinds of lips. You can draw fuller or smaller lips. I wanted to draw a bit of the teeth to show you how to draw teeth. The lower lip should be placed exactly in the middle between the bottom of the nose and chin.

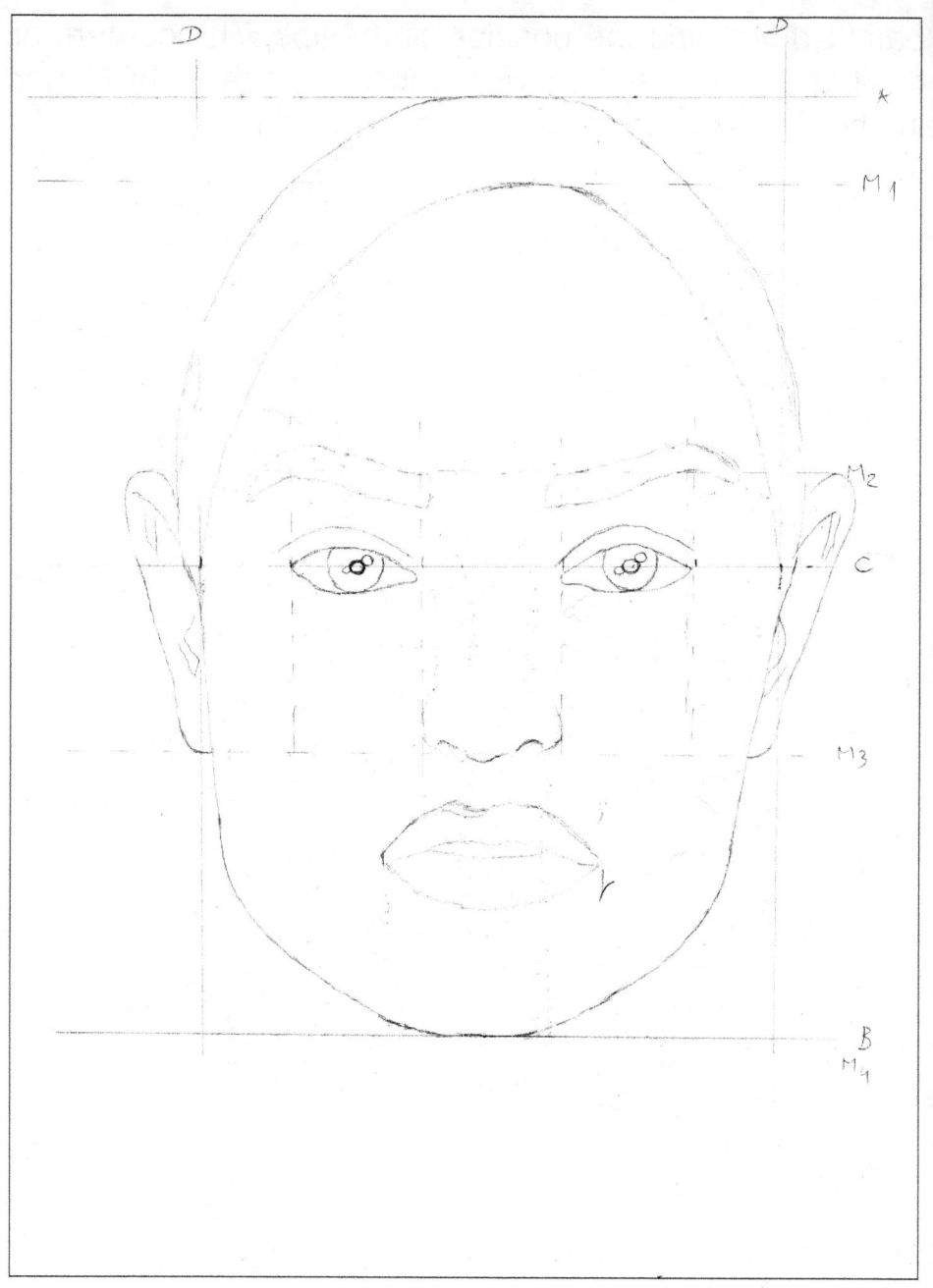

Now you can either erase the grid lines and draw over this paper, or trace this outline on another sheet of paper. Here you can change anything that you want and add some details, but, of course, it can be changed during the drawing progress. I have drawn my sketch on a clean piece of paper since my paper was damaged by erasing as I moved the ruler and my hand over. I have omitted some lines that are not necessary that were double lines, as I was trying to find the right position. So, draw only the lines that you find necessary.

Now you can start using a piece of paper or a tissue to hold your hand on in order to avoid direct contact between the skin and the paper. This will also avoid smudging of the already drawn and shaded areas.

So, let's focus on a single facial feature at a time.

Let's start with the eyes, which are the most important facial feature. You can either draw the eyes one by one, or – like me - both at the same time.

Using an 8B, or any other pencil darker than 4B, fill the pupils. Pupils can be on the larger or smaller side; draw them just the way you want. I have chosen a normal size. An 8B is a very dark pencil, which is what we need for the pupils. I will always use an 8B for the darkest tones throughout this tutorial because I have only this one from 4B-9B. However, as I mentioned in the "Tools" chapter, you can use any of the other darker tones.

Draw the pupils carefully with a well-sharpened pencil to keep the circles perfect and fill the paper completely.

In the next image you can see my freshly drawn sketch and pupils though you will find the zoomed images in the following steps so that you can see the details better.

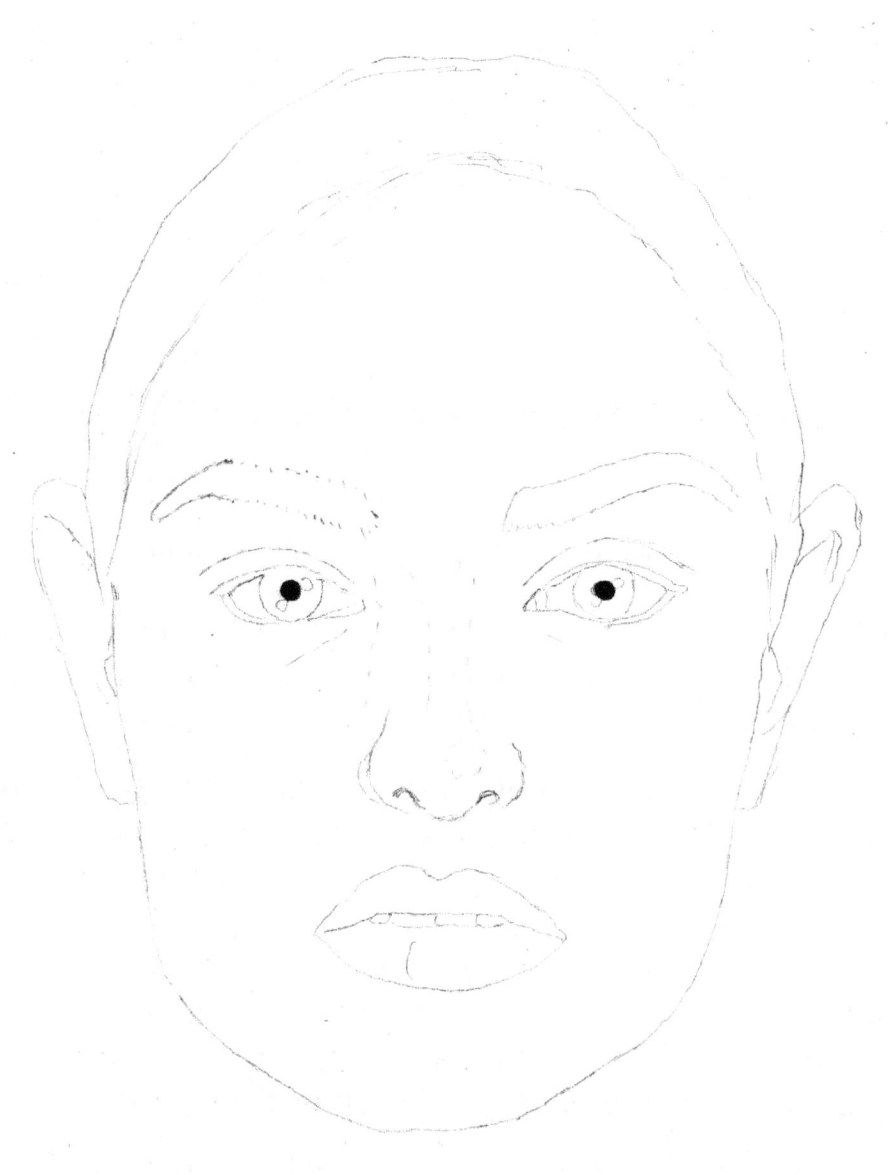

For the next step let's just outline the iris boundary. Use a B pencil for this: it should be a very sharp pencil. Make the outline about 1mm thick, if you draw on the A4 paper size, like me. Press lightly in the lower area, and press harder under the upper eyelid. Try to preserve the perfect round circle of the iris boundary, even if you haven't sketched out perfect circle or and you think it's not good, here you can improve. So, sketch is important, but not as important as shading and highlighting. Don't forget to skip the upper part of the iris since we want it covered with the upper eyelid. The upper area should always be much darker than the lower area.

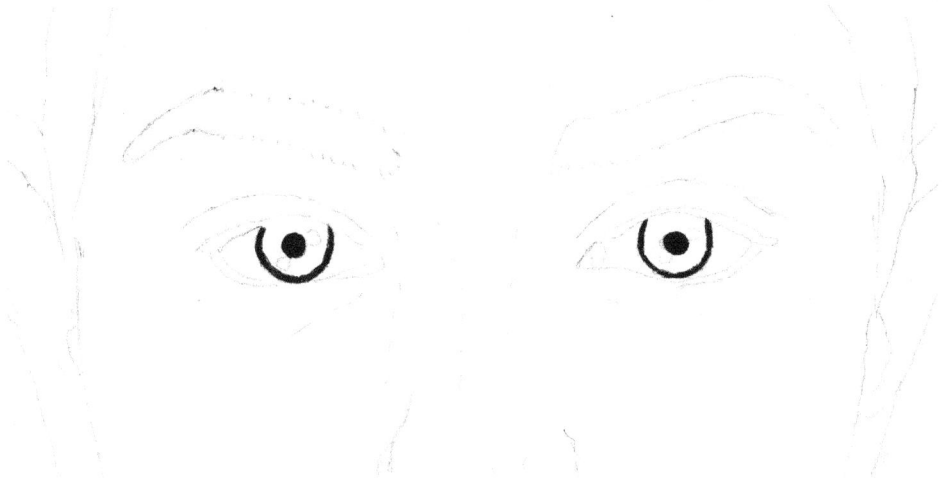

Create the shadow over the upper areas of the iris that is cast by the upper eyelid. Use a B pencil for this and press very hard. This cast shadow should be big, it can even reach the pupil, depending on so many things. Don't forget to skip the light reflections if you have created some and just draw around them. Always study the image that follows the instruction to see what I want to explain before you start drawing the step.

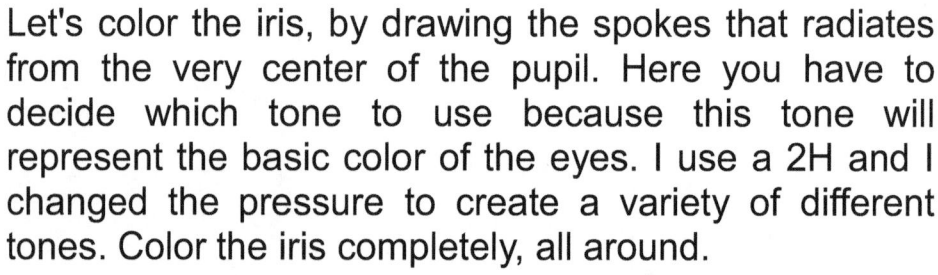

Let's color the iris, by drawing the spokes that radiates from the very center of the pupil. Here you have to decide which tone to use because this tone will represent the basic color of the eyes. I use a 2H and I changed the pressure to create a variety of different tones. Color the iris completely, all around.

Press a bit harder next to the iris boundary and of course skip the reflected light; wherever you have it drawn, just draw around it. Also, press harder in the upper area because it is always less illuminated. Even better, use an HB. If you have exaggerated with shading, or the iris is too dark, you can just eliminate it with an eraser. You can always lighten it up if you have made it too dark. You can add much more details, but this is pretty small drawing, no point in adding such small details. I have a tutorial on a single eye, which is a pretty big eye, and I could then go much more into detail, so you can check it out.

You can see in the next image that by leaving out the area for light reflection you make the eyes appear shinier.

On this portrait, everything should be colored except for the light reflections. So, we have to shade the whites of the eyes too. We have to determine where the light source is coming from. I want it to come from the upper-right corner of the paper, and we have to shade the whole drawing according to this. Shade the Sclera, the white of the eyes, using 2H in the corners on the left side. These areas have to be the darkest because they don't receive much light. It is so-called self-shadow. Use circular motions, pressing gently and blend it with a Q-tip or a blending stump, but use a clear tip of it, and not the one that you used for shading before.

Create the cast shadow under the upper eyelid the same way. This shading will suggest the roundness of the eyeball so we just have to improvise it by creating a gradient transition between the tones.

Shade less in the corners on the right sides, but create a stronger shadow that is cast by the upper eyelid because here the eyelashes are denser. Don't forget to shade tear ducts with a 2H and blend it with a blending stump. You don't have to press too hard, but rather make slow progress. Press less, and you will see if you have to shade it more. Just go over it again and again until you achieve a very good tone. Actually, you'll see at the end of the drawing when everything is finished, whether you need to shade the sclera more. But for now, shade them normally.

Shade the visible thickness of the skin of the lower eyelid too, using a blending stump that you already used for shading some darker areas, so that it has some graphite on its tip.

Before we start drawing eyelashes, let's shade the skin around the eyes because the eyelashes should be applied after that.

First, use an HB to darken the crease.

Now start shading the skin around the eyes before we apply eyelashes. So, if we have our light source coming from the upper-right corner, the left eye should be a bit darker everywhere.

Let's shade the left areas first, between the eye and crease. This way you can understand that the left side is always much darker than if you focused on one eye at a time.

Use a B pencil for the left eye, and an HB for the right eye. Start on the very left side (above the outer corner and above the tear duct). Draw the strokes towards the middle area pressing hard on the left side and release the pressure as you draw towards the highlights in the middle.

Blend this all with a Q-tip. You can always add more shade if necessary. Every time when you blend, you will remove a bit of graphite, so just shade again what you have removed.

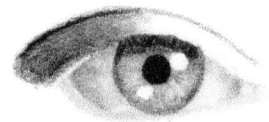
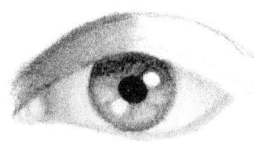

Do the same, but starting from the right sides. Use an HB for the left eye and a 2H for the right eye, and also release the pressure us you reach the mid area, the highlights, somewhere in the center, above the iris. Shade the highlights too, but use a 6H, pressing lightly and blend it with a clean Q-tip. We have to shade even the brightest areas. Even if some area is pretty bright, you shouldn't think that it doesn't have any shade.

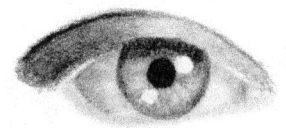
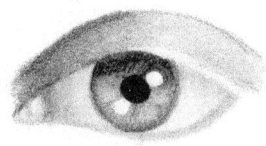

Use a 4B to strengthen the left crease because probably you have removed a bit of graphite with a Q-tip, so apply that again. The crease above the left eye should be much darker than the crease above the right eye.

For the right crease, use an HB to strengthen it. Also, strengthen the lower outline of the eyebrows, so that you can have them more visible.

Let's shade the area between the crease and eyebrows first. We have to shade this area too before the eyelashes because we can draw maybe longer eyelashes, but some of them will definitely reach this area. So, we can just create the whole skin, hardest part. Start over the left area of the right eye, using and HB, circular motions all the time. Don't press very hard, but rather try to make a slow progress. This area above the tear duct should be a bit darker than the next area closer to the temple, that should be a very highlighted area. Of course, in the case of the left eye, that area should be in the shadow. Press harder next to the crease line in order to make that gradient transition between the crease and tone of the skin, using circular motion. The circular motion is the best for the skin. We will be practicing this a lot later when we're going to completely shade the skin. I wouldn't recommend using strokes or cross hatches for the skin, but, of course, some may prefer to draw with them. But, that's a different kind of method than what I use to create.

Blend the area with a Q-tip to make the area look smoother. A blending stump is too small for this and can leave some visible, thick lines, so Q-tip or a tissue are much better for blending larger areas.

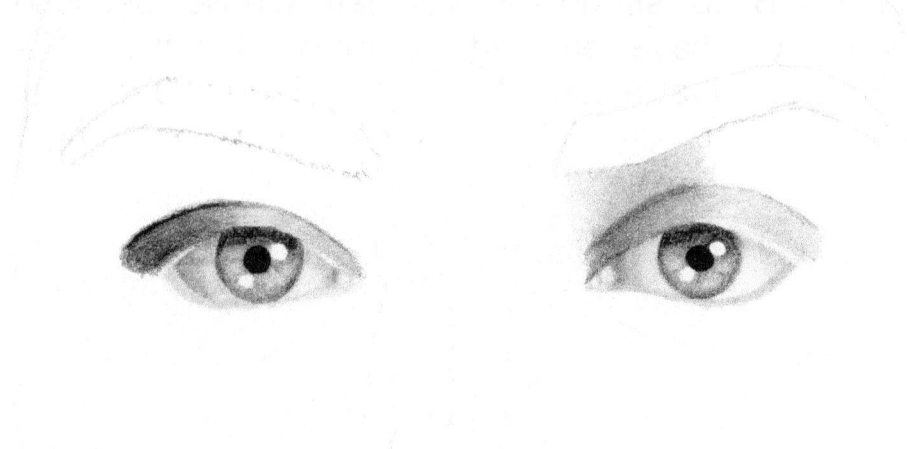

Now we can shade the right side above the crease, using a 2H, pressing hard in the middle and releasing the pressure as we approach the highlight under the arched part of the eyebrow, on the right side. Blend it all with a tissue.

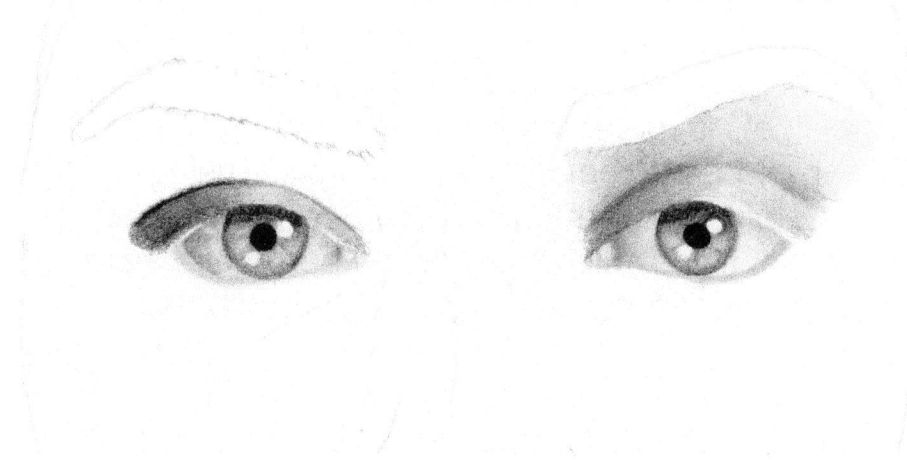

Shade the left eye now, but keep in mind this area should be very dark. If we have our light source coming from the upper-right corner of the paper, shade the areas hidden from the light more, as shown in the next image. Use an HB, make circular motions and press harder. The area right above the crease should be shaded pretty much, so here also press harder with an HB. An HB is pretty dark, so don't go with a darker choice because you can still make a dark tone with a HB. You can see which area I have left for the brighter skin.

Blend it all with a Q-tip and strengthen the crease with a 4B or darker, if necessary. Create the gradient transition above the crease to suggest the roundness of this upper area.

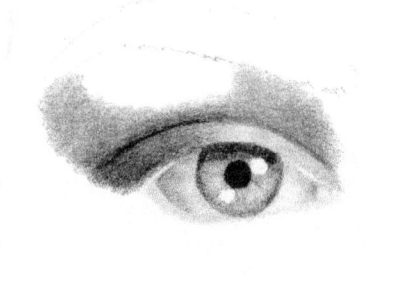 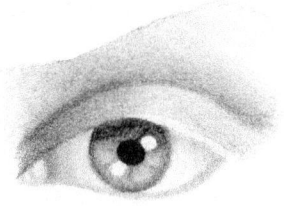

Finish shading this area under the eyebrow, using an HB. Press less and less as you approach the arched part of the eyebrow, and here too, the gradient transition between the grey tones is very important. This area is also highlighted, but it's still pretty dark, so use an HB the whole time and change the pressure. Blend it all with a Q-tip or a tissue and improve on the gradient transition with a pencil, if necessary. Then you blend again until it's flawless. If you have shaded too much, just remove it with an eraser. Sometimes, it is enough to blend with a tissue and may also eliminate some of the graphite. You can always lighten it up.

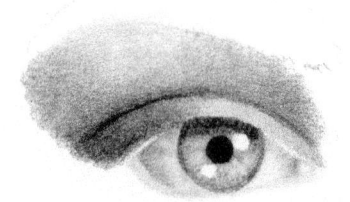 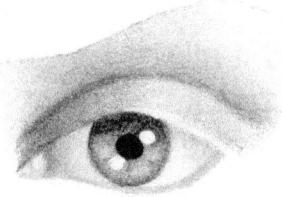

If you're satisfied with these shaded areas, you can draw eyelashes.

Start with the vertical eyelashes in the very middle, above the iris since they are the simplest to draw. Use a 4B or darker for the eyelashes. Of course, you can use even brighter tones if you want. Some of the eyelashes should be shorter, some longer. Add a bit of cast shadow over the iris, if necessary. Create thick line over the roots of the eyelashes to create self-shadow and shadow cast by eyelashes.

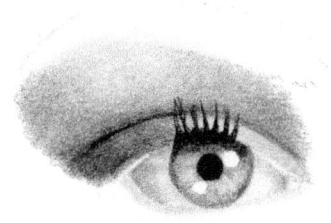 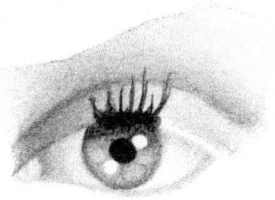

Now, start drawing the eyelashes towards the tear duct. Make them less dense, shorter and brighter. Draw a bit downwards, and then horizontally towards the tear duct, then just make them curve a bit upwards. The tinier eyelashes next to the tear duct should be drawn horizontally. Also, shade the thick line between the sclera and the skin above.

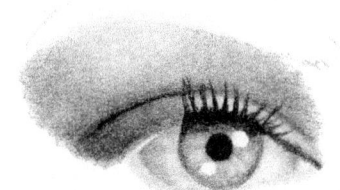 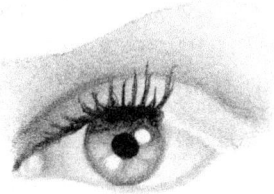

Create the longer eyelashes towards the temples. Draw them a bit downwards, and then start curving them towards the temple. Make them at random, they shouldn't be the same size nor should they go in the same direction. Draw longer and longer eyelashes as you work towards the outer corners of the eyes. They should also progressively get more dense and thick. After having drawn the eyelashes, you can see if the sclera is too bright or too dark, so can remove some shade, or shade more. It will be even more apparent at the end of the drawing, when we have drawn the surrounding area completely.

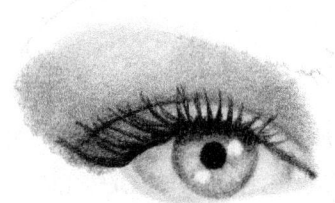 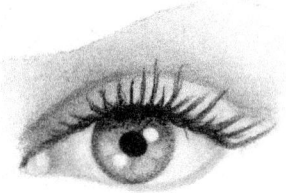

Now we can shade the areas under both eyes using an HB in circular motion. This is necessary so that we can draw eyelashes here too and then move forward. Shade right under the thickness of the skin, over that circular muscle, going all around the eye. The area in the middle should be left highlighted. Press much harder under the left eye. Referring to our light source in the upper-right corner, the areas on the left sides should be shaded more, so you can use a B pencil for the area under the outer corner of the left eye. The area under the right eye should be brighter. Try to cover the areas evenly.

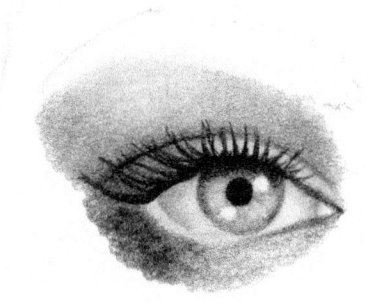
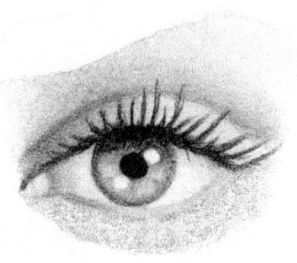

Blend it all with a Q-tip, also using circular motions and carefully blending everything that you have shaded. You will see how it becomes very smooth after blending, which is amazing. These Q-tips are very good for areas like this, areas that are neither too big nor too small. Tissues are good for a bit of a larger area. You can add details if you want more details.

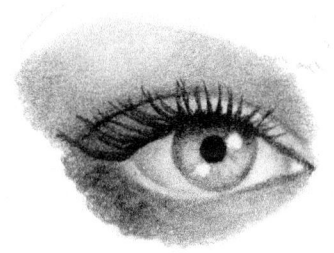
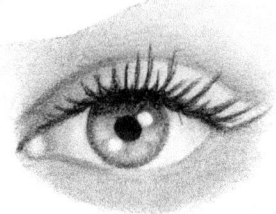

Now we can draw eyelashes. Next to the tear ducts draw very short, tiny eyelashes that should become bigger, longer and denser as you draw them towards the outer corners of the eyes. I'm using an HB for these eyelashes because the lower eyelashes should be a bit brighter than the upper eyelashes; they are always thinner. Make some of their ends meet, creating the shape of tents. Some of the eyelashes should grow a bit under the edge between the thickness of the skin and the skin under it. You should check for reference photos, or look in the mirror to check up for their position. Use a B pencil, or even darker, for the eyelashes under the outer corner of the left eye.

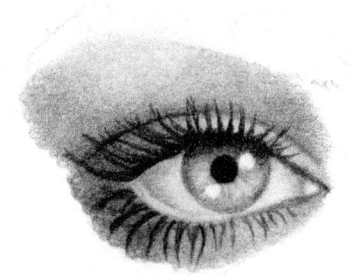 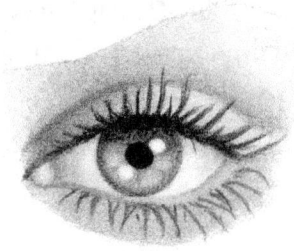

In this step we can do some finishing touches to make it better, but of course, you can do it at the end of the drawing if you so choose. I just wanted to show you how you can create a bit of highlight with an eraser or a white marker in the middle, right under the iris boundary and over the tear ducts to suggest the wetness of the eyes. In the next image, you can see how the eyes now appear more shiny.

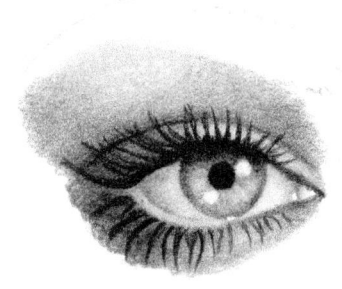 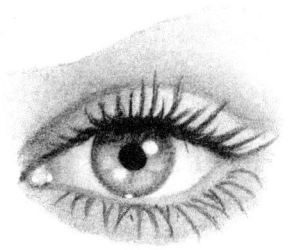

Now, we can draw the eyebrows. In the next image you can see the arrowed lines that I have digitally placed to show you the direction and position of the hairs that you should draw.

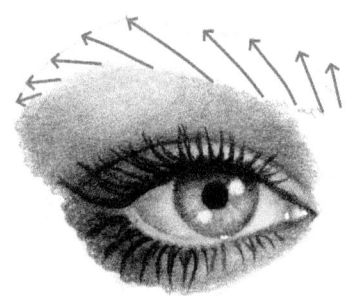 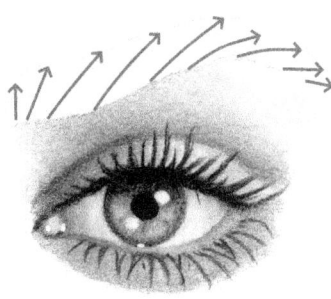

Refer to this image all the time and draw thinner and shorter eyebrows as you move towards the temple. Use an HB for the right eyebrow and keep drawing in the direction of these arrows. The eyebrows can be thicker, thinner, or any shape, but the direction of the hair growth is actually the same, no matter what, and you should follow these rules if you want to draw photorealistic drawings.

When you are drawing them over the arch make sure to press a bit less on the highlighted area. Here we have horizontal lines and you make them curved again as you draw towards the temple. You should press harder again next to the temple. I have made the brows a bit thicker because I want to make them more visible and more eye-catching, but you can make thin eyebrows if you'd like.

For the left eyebrow, use a B pencil, and also pres less over the protruding area.

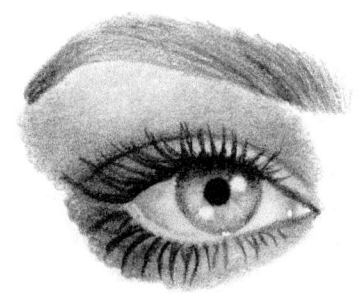 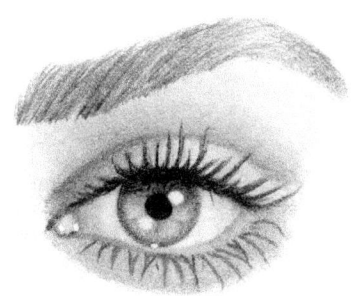

Blend them a bit with a blending stump. Try to keep the tip of your blending stump within an area of the eyebrows. Don't blend much outside of the edge. You can see in the next image how they appear much softer after blending.

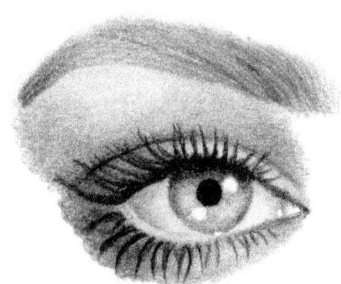
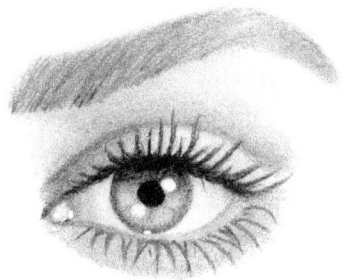

In the next step, we can add some highlighted hairs over the protruding parts, mostly in the upper areas of the eyebrows. Use a sharp point of your erase r and erase the illuminated hairs also following the direction of those arrows.

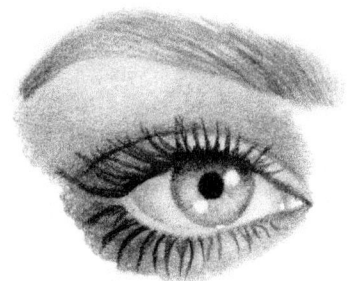
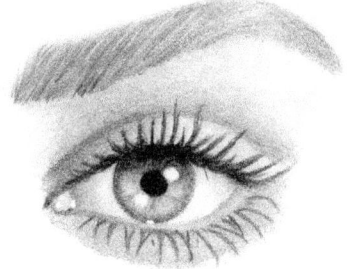

Lastly, we can create the darkest parts in the lower horizontal half of the eyebrows because these areas get less light. Use a pencil 2B-4B and cover the lower half of the hairs completely. Also, draw some of the dark hairs in the upper area too. At random, mostly among the highlighted hairs. If you draw a male, you can add additional, tiny hairs out of the outline of the eyebrows, particularly next to the temple. As always, check up for the reference photos, or study the facial features on your friends and family members.

If you stand away from your drawing and look at it from a distance, you will see how visible the highlights are, how strong the shadows are, and how they relate to each other. So, you can see many things that you can't see when you look at them from a closer distance.

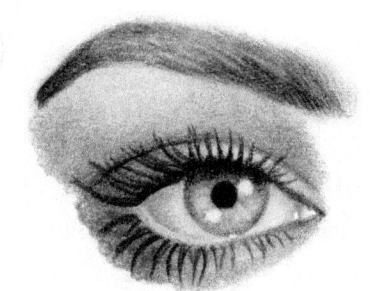 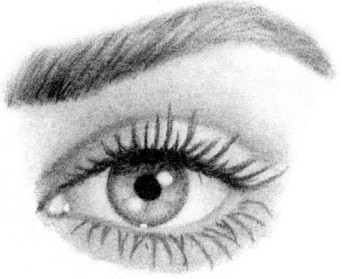

We can now move to the nose.

Mark the nostrils and cast a shadow on the left side of the left nostril, using a 4B or darker. Also, strengthen the line under the nose and keep in mind the light source when shading the nose. You will probably have to strengthen these shadows later on because you will have to blend it all and graphite will be eliminated. Nostrils sometimes cannot be visible, depending on the kind of the nose you wish to draw.

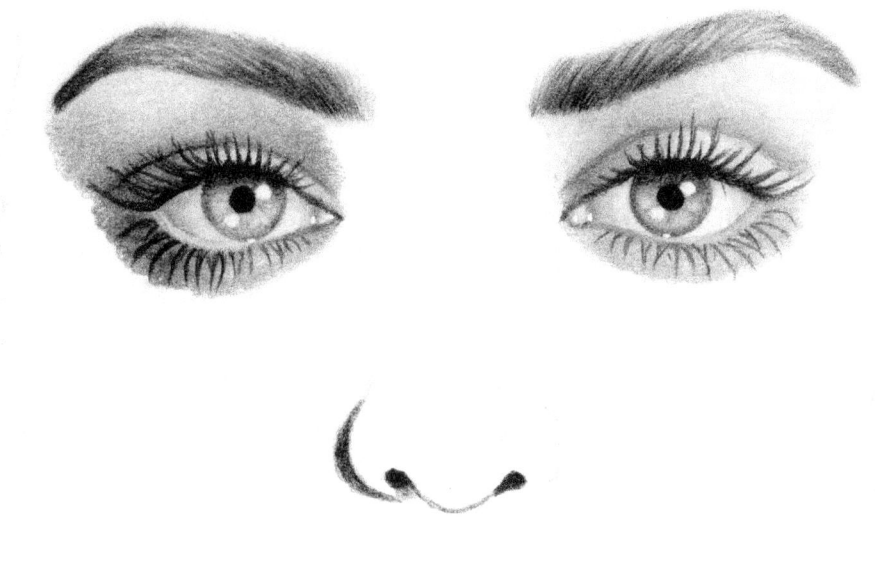

The next step is to shade the whole, shadowed area on the left side and under the nose. Use an HB, press very hard in the areas that can receive less light, and release the pressure as you shade towards the more illuminated areas. Study my next image to see which areas I have shaded. This is very time consuming work and you should take your time. An HB is very good because you can create a variety of tones from 2B to 5H only by changing the pressure on the pencil. This is probably why it got the name HB since you can use it as both. Of course, it can't create as dark a tone as 8B, for example, but it's a must-have pencil because it can replace many of them.

Keep using circular motion to create a smoother texture. Take a look at the next image to see how visible my tiny, overlapping circles are. But no worries, we are going to blend the areas and they will look even smoother. Just please don't use strokes or cross hatches. I know they would take less time, but the result would be disappointing. As with so many things in life, more time spent on work will yield better results.

The size of the area that we shade in this step depends on the size of the nose and the source of the light that falls over the face. In this step, do not do any gradient transition because we're going to do that later. I have split this work into smaller actions, to make you focus on the one thing at a time.

Leave the outer edge of the left rim untouched because here we have to create a reflected light. Just draw around it as you can see in the next image. Do the same on the bottom of the nose and shade the self-shadow above it. The self-shadow and reflected light under it will suggest a roundness of the nose and actually will separate it from the face.

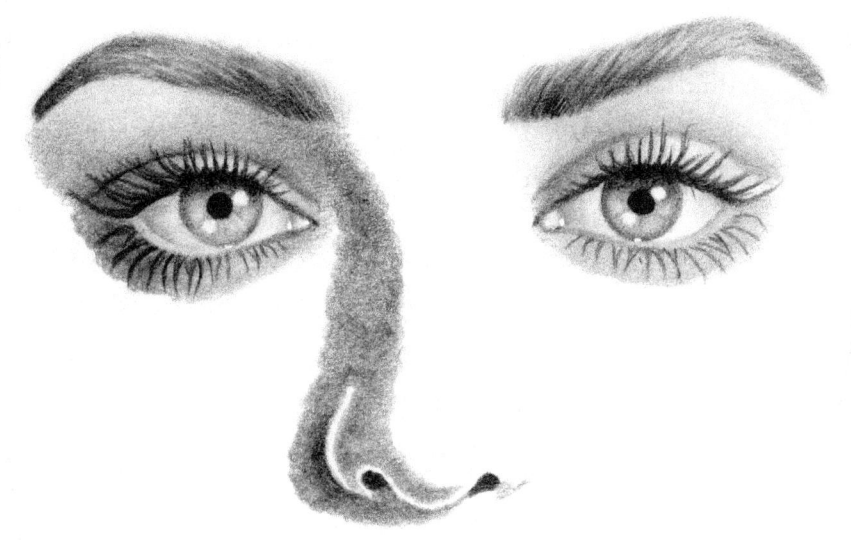

Now switch to 2H and shade all around the previously shaded area. Same circular motion, pressing hard over the edge of the HB area and release the pressure as you work away from it because we have to create a gradient transition from the very dark tone to the basic tone of the skin. When I say the basic color of the skin, I mean the skin tone which is not affected by the light, yet not found in shadow. In the next image, you can already see how the top of the nose appears round due to this gradient transition, which is always very important.

The darker shadow next to the rim is a shadow cast by the nostril which we shaded in the previous step. Using a 2H, shade further from the nose over the lower-left area under it to create the shadow cast by the top of the nose. This will be much further from the nose and also brighten the shadow cast very close to the nose. It will say that the top of the nose is closer to the viewers eye than the rims of the nose. This distance is not too big, but we still have to improvise it. Do not make sudden progress, but go over the same area again and again still using circular motions. Keep in mind that once you apply 2H or a similar bright tone, you won't be able to make it absolutely dark again, even if you go over it with a 4B or darker. That's why it is important to use a very dark pencil first for the areas that are supposed to be in the shadow.

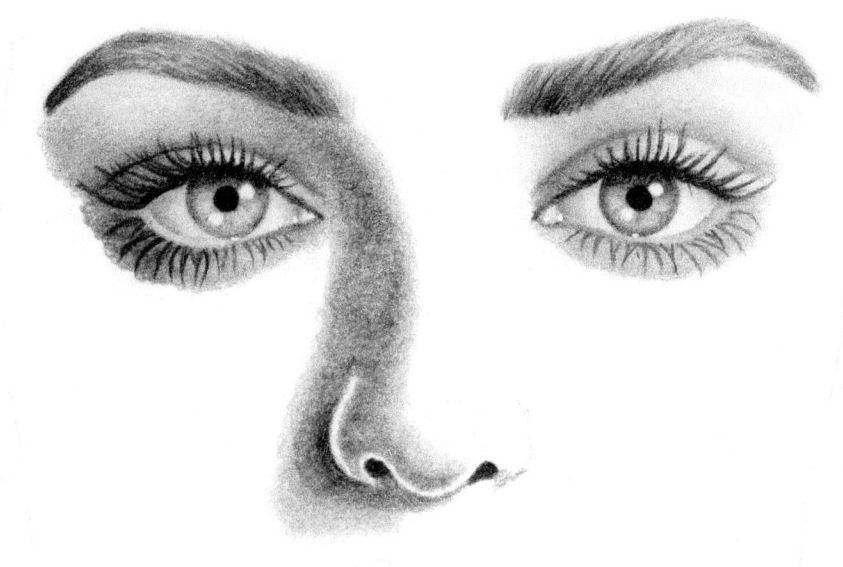

The next thing to do is to shade around the previously shaded area in the same manner, pressing harder next to this area, releasing the pressure as you shade away from it, using a 4H. You can still use 2H if you'd like but press less. You should use a dull tip of any of the H pencils because they can scratch your paper if they are sharp. With a dull tip, you can create very bright areas without scratching the paper.

Leave untouched the highlight over the top of the nose - as shown in the next image – just shade around the tiny dot. Press harder between the rim on the right side and the top of the nose. Also, shade the whole left side of the bridge, still using a 4H. I'm trying to use a single pencil in each step, so that you can understand it better.

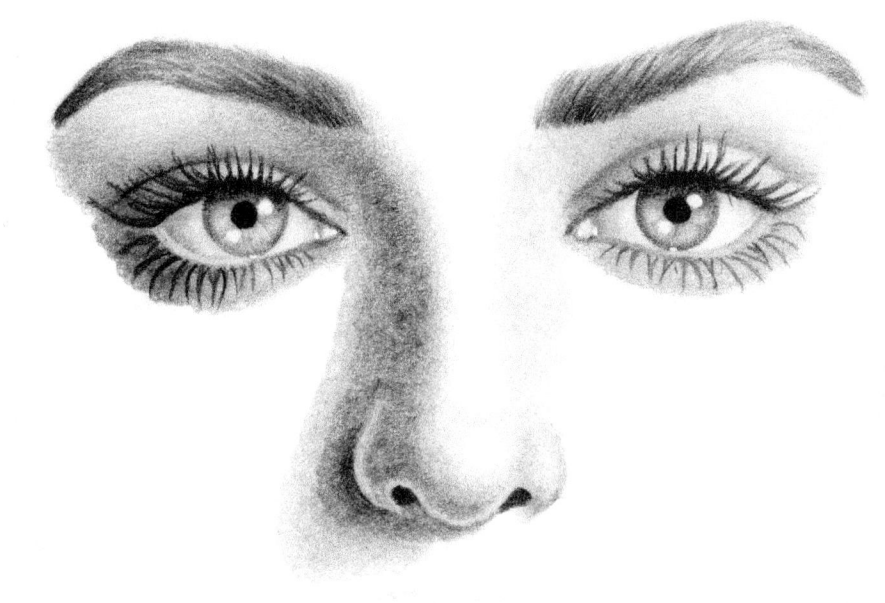

Now, blend it all. Use a Q-tip to blend the left side, which is darker, but use a clean piece of a tissue to blend the brighter areas on the right side. Press hard to fill the tooth of the paper with the graphite. You can see how much smoother the shaded area is now after blending. You can hardly see the tiny, overlapping circles that were pretty visible before blending.

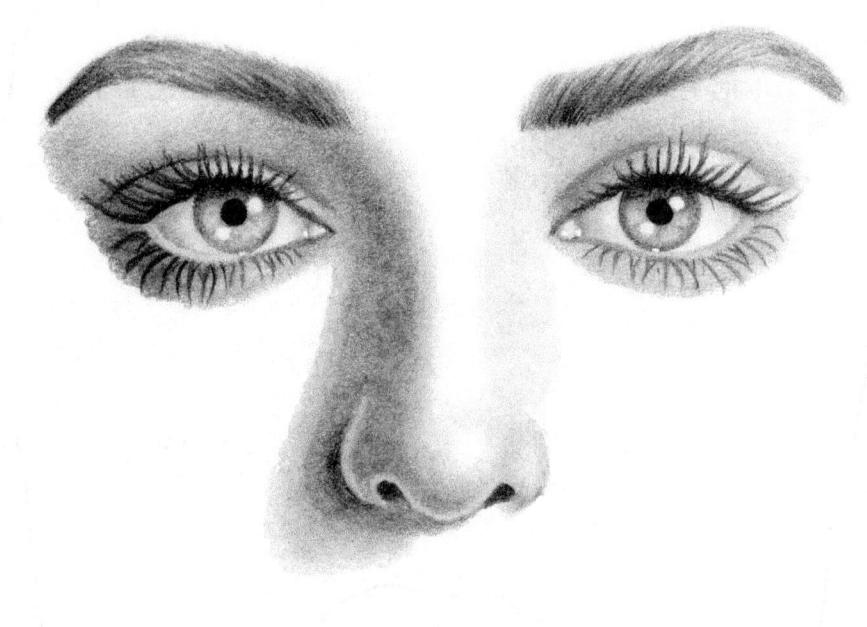

Now shade the rest of the face except for the highlighted areas: the white dot over the top of the nose that we left untouched, and along the bridge of the nose as shown in the next image.

Use a 6H in circular motions and blend it all with a clean piece of a tissue. Press harder next to the edge of the darker tone and keep the circular motion. Actually, nothing should be absolutely white, unless if the skin is wet. Then it should be glossy and we would have absolutely white highlights, but otherwise, it should be covered. Don't forget that you can always easily remove bright shades with an eraser, and make highlight brighter if you have exaggerated shaded it.

As you can see I still have some imperfections as I use a circular motion but this is actually the normal skin. There are always some tiny wrinkles and moles, not to mention the older person's skin, it is not so smooth. Make gradient transitions between the highlights and maybe not that kind of basic skin tone.

Darken more the area that you shade in the first step of drawing the nose because you have probably removed a bit of the graphite as you shaded it with a Q-tip. Use an HB, pressing hard in circular motions. Also, darken the reflected light on the rim and under the nose, if necessary.

In this step shade the area between the eyebrows, still using a 6H, pressing harder, or switch to a 4B. This area should be a bit darker than the forehead because there is a protruding frontal bone above it and we have to shade more that self-shadow. Blend it with a clean Q-tip.

In the next image, you can see that actually the cast shadows and reflected light is what changes it from a two-dimensional to three-dimensional picture.

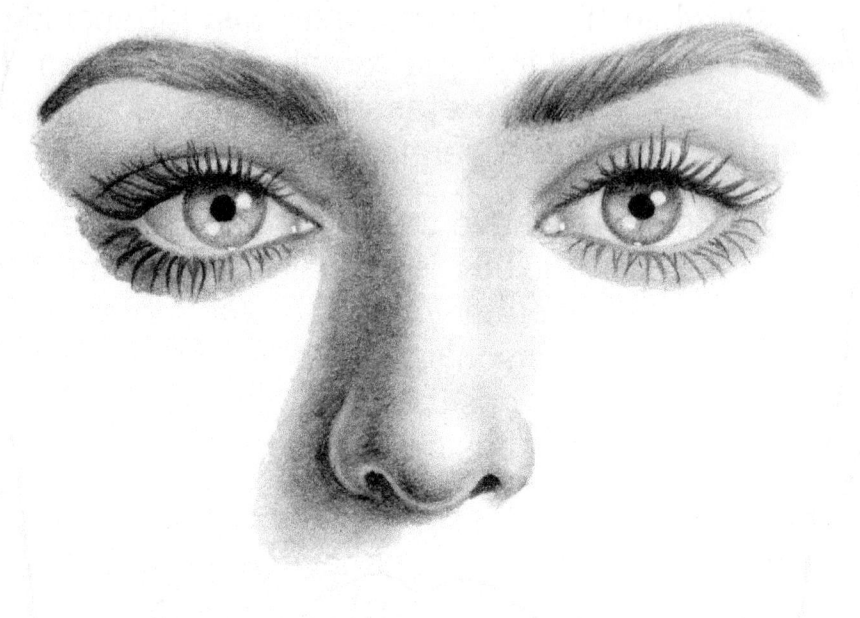

You can always shade more or brighten up the highlights, even at the end of the drawing. You can change the shape of anything by changing the tone of the shadows and highlights. Just think about the make-up artists that make the nose thinner, the face thinner, or the cheeks fuller. It's always shadows and highlights that will make the changes, so you can change the entire face shape and appearance by just moving the position of the highlights and shadows a bit. The shadows and highlights are crucial, but of course we have to have the proportional sketch to have the facial features drawn on their natural places as they normally appear.

As you are shading, for example, the left side of the

nose, the vertical highlight will become more prominent. So, if you want to enhance highlight, but you can't make it brighter, or it is bright but still not bright enough because surrounding areas are too bright, just shade around the highlights - more or less - and they will become brighter.

If you apply brighter tones first such as 2H or brighter, you won't be able to make that area absolute black anymore. For example, if you shade an area with a 5H and you apply a 6B over it, a 6B won't create as dark tone as when applied as a first layer on the paper. Sometimes you would want it to happen, but sometimes you wouldn't. So, this is a very useful thing to know.

How to Draw Lips

Let's move to the lips now, and we are done with the facial features.

I want to draw the teeth too, but you don't have to if you don't want. I just want to show you how to draw them in the case that you want them visible in your future portraits. I want to draw teeth, but not a smile, just a slightly opened mouth.

In this first step, I'm just strengthening all the lines that I created and have also added the lines between the teeth. The teeth shouldn't stay absolutely white, particularly when they are hardly visible. When you draw a smile, only the front teeth can stay white. As you work on the rest of the teeth, use darker and darker tones as you shade them towards the corners. This way the teeth will have their round shape and the smile will look more realistic.

I used an 8B to darken the area between the teeth. Of course, there is a tongue behind, but it gets no light at all, so we can use the darkest tone for this. You can create different shapes of the teeth. If you want to make them stick to each other, just use an HB to create the lines between them.

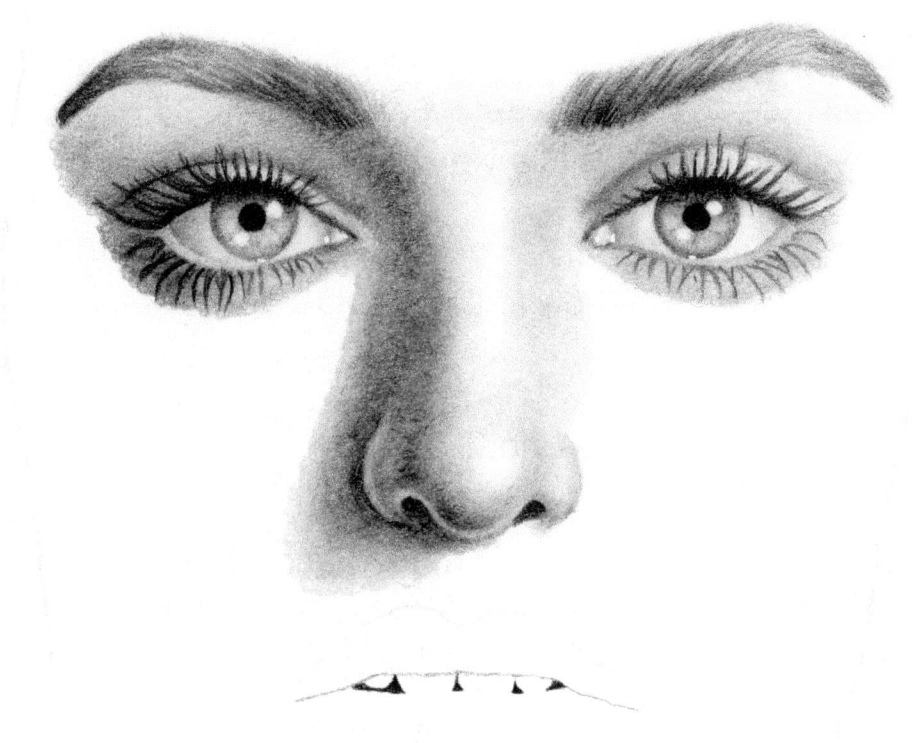

Shade the teeth with a 6H, applying circular motions. Press a bit harder under the upper lip. In the next image, you can see still that the teeth I just shaded are not white anymore, yet they are bright enough that they suggest the whiteness of the teeth, but in the shadow. After we have drawn the surrounding areas, lips, it will enhance the whiteness of the teeth even more, so don't hesitate to shade them well.

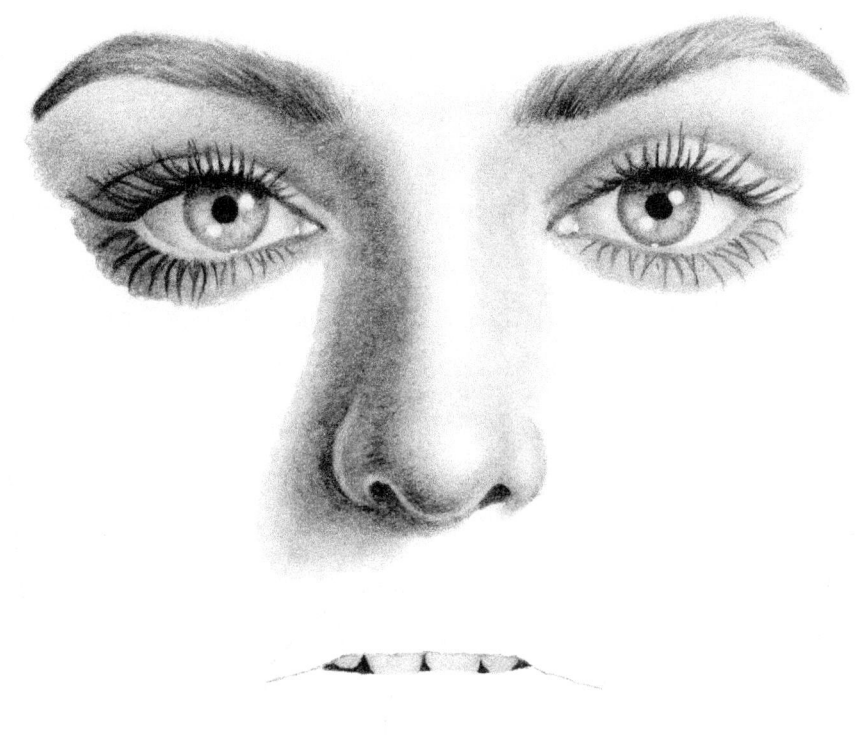

Let's divide this task into two parts and draw the two lips separately, starting with the upper lip.

I'm using a B pencil in the lower horizontal half of the upper lip, as shown in the next image. You can leave out the lower edge untouched for the reflected light. So, the area that we shade here is so-called self-shadow. Press a bit less in the right corner because we have our light source coming from the upper-right corner.

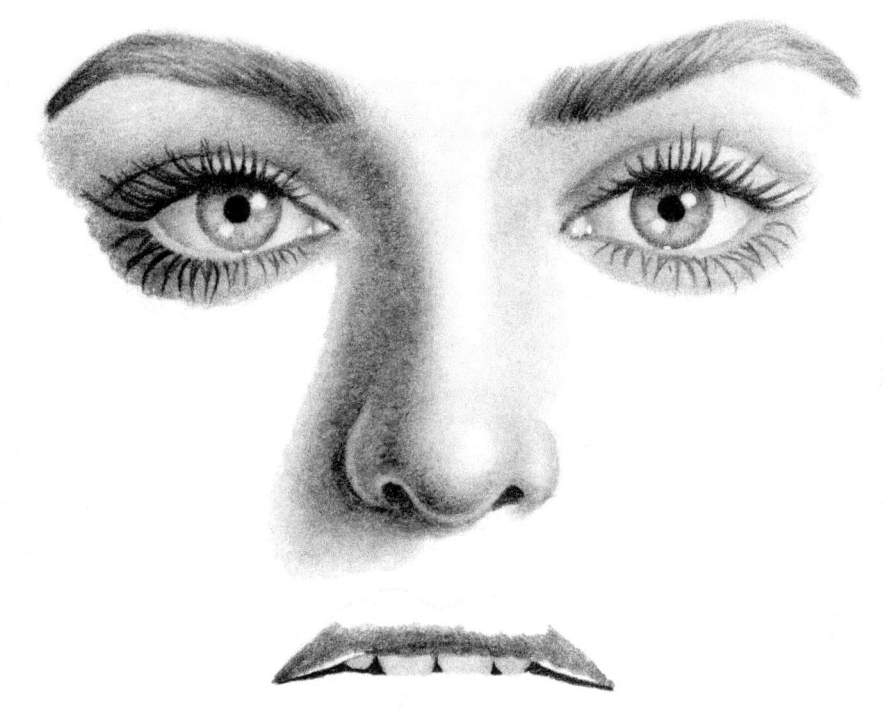

The upper area can be shaded with an HB. Here you have to decide what kind of shape you want. It can be any shape, you don't have to draw exactly like me. Don't press too hard when shading this area with an HB, but only next to the lower area that we shaded.

Press harder, and press less and less as you shade upwards. Here also, that gradient transition is important to improvise the roundness of the lip, and that's why this HB is good for the area next to a B pencil.

I want to draw lips with a bit of lipstick on them and that's why I'm using darker tones, but you can use a bit brighter, an HB for the lower area and a 2H in upper area.

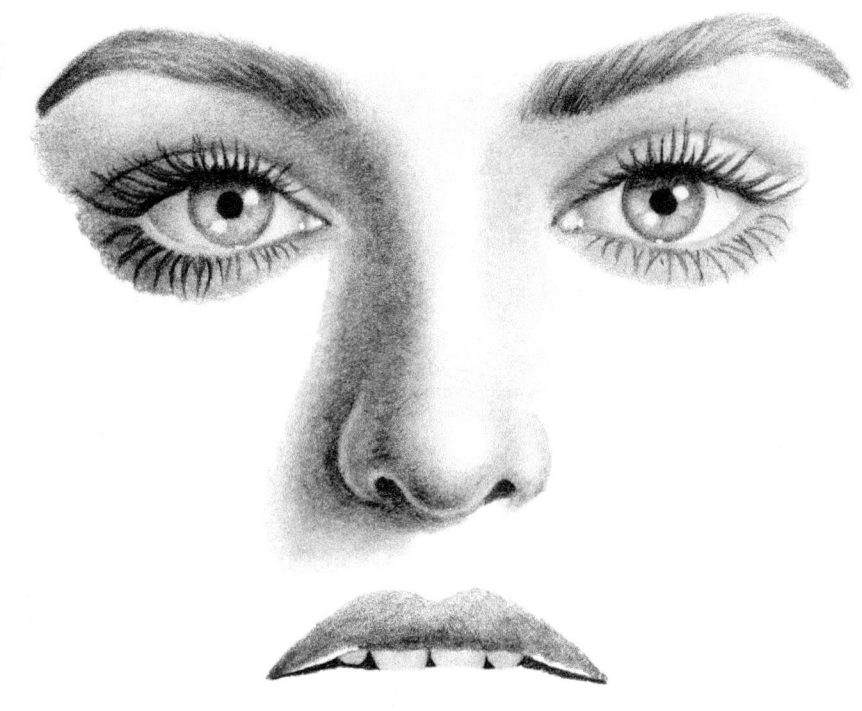

Blend it all with a Q-tip. In the next image, you can see how it now looks very good and smooth after blending.

If you shade out of the edge, it's not even a problem because we're going to shade the skin around the lips.

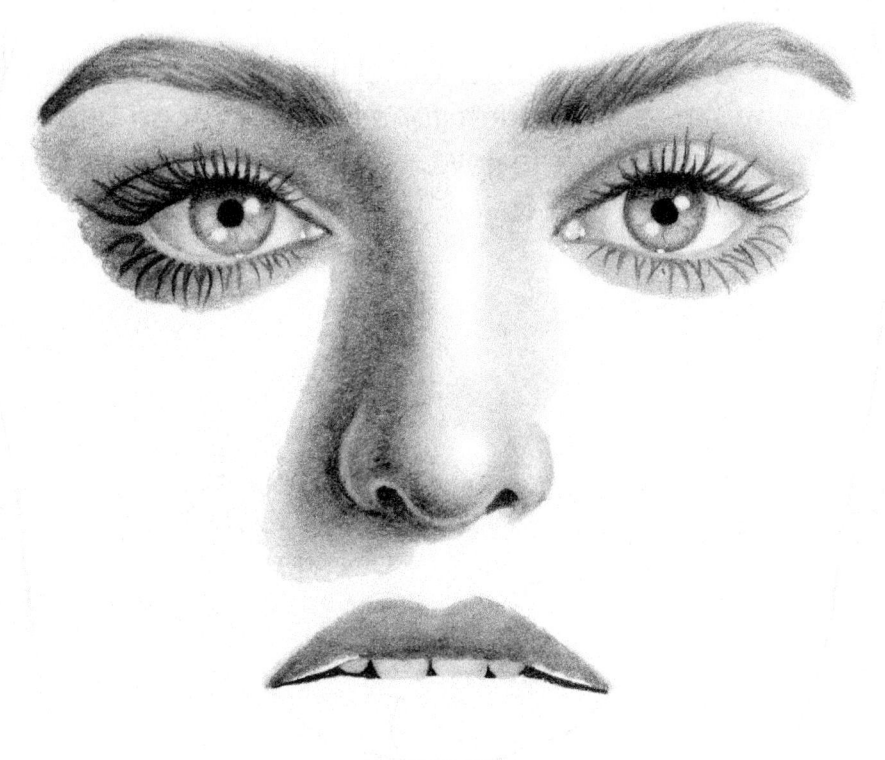

Shade the reflected light that you left untouched, using a 6H. The reflected light shouldn't stay white, and should actually be pretty dark, yet much brighter than the surrounding areas. Create the reflected light above the teeth too. The reflected light will suggest glossiness of the lips because the dry lips don't really have too much visibly reflected light. Erase the tiny line, 1mm above the edge above the teeth. The reflected light will also suggest the roundness of the lip.

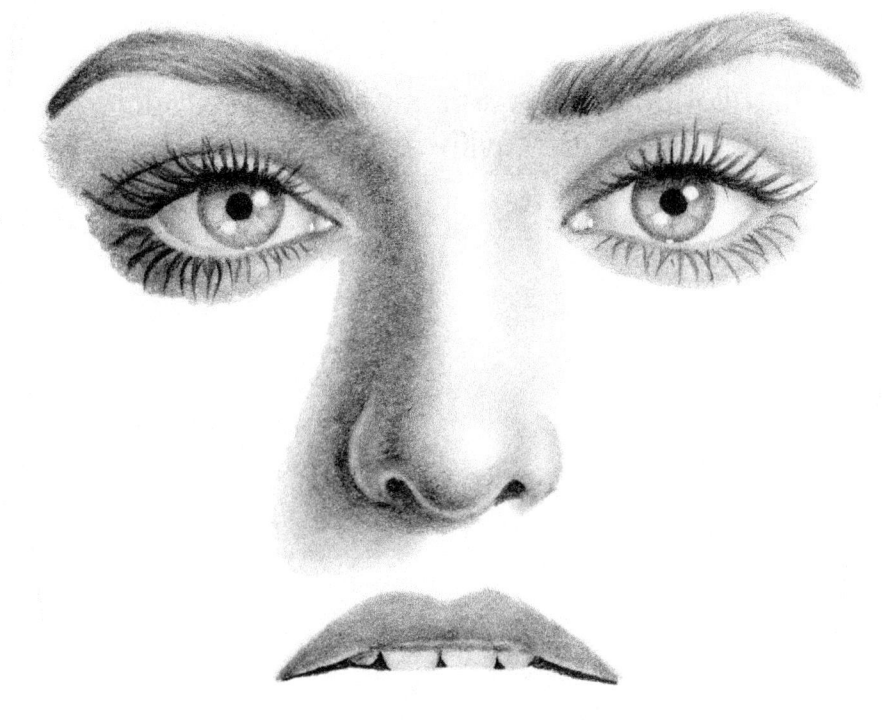

In this step, create some highlights over the upper area of the upper lip, so just use an eraser and gently eliminate a bit of the graphite. Work right under the edge, also leaving 1 mm between the Cupid's bow and this highlight. If you exaggerate with erasing, just go over the too bright area with a used tip of the blending stump to apply some of the graphite again, and it won't be too bright anymore.

You can also create some highlights between the wrinkles. The lip should be more illuminated on the right side and less on the left side due to the light source that's coming from the upper-right corner. Yet, make some highlights on the left side by just touching the surface of the paper   with an eraser, so don't press hard.

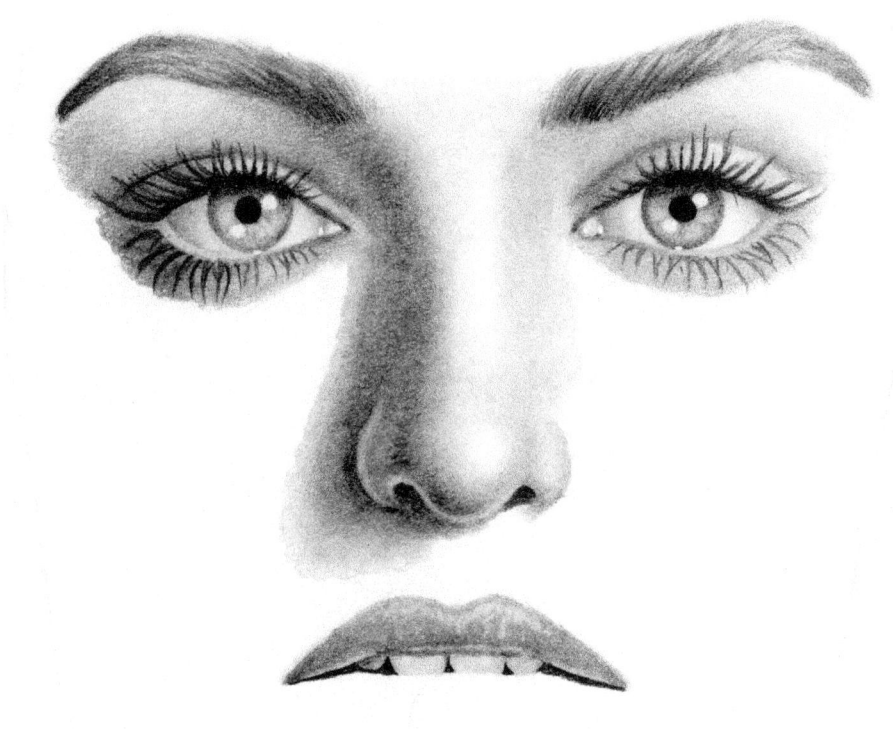

Now we can finish this upper lip by adding some shadows. I'm using an 8B to strengthen the self-shadow that I have eliminated with blending and creating the wrinkles between the highlights. Make these wrinkles radiate from the center of the lips. They shouldn't be too dark, but just try to make them visible. In the very middle of the lips, we have to draw a vertical wrinkle. The others should be curved.

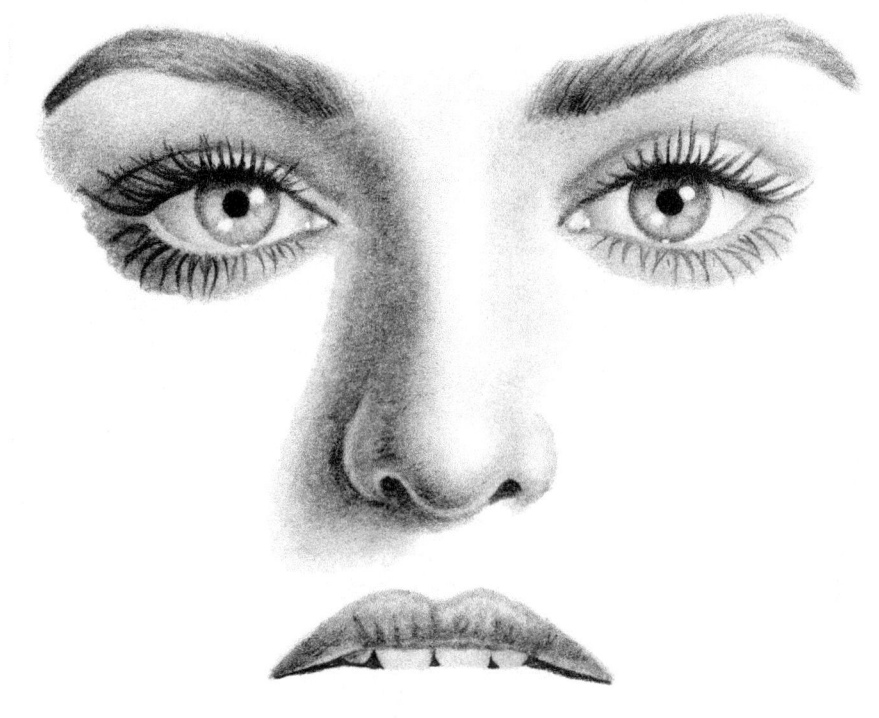

It's time for the lower lip, which should be quite brighter than the upper lip because it is always more illuminated. Start with the areas that get less light, as shown in the next image, using a B pencil. Fill the upper area, right under the teeth and leave untouched the highlighted area in the middle.

Still using a B pencil, press harder on the left side of the lower lip because it would receive a small amount of light if the light source is found in the upper-right corner.

Also, shade the lower edge of the lower lip, something like a 2mm thick edge that you can see in the next image. The lower lip can be any other shape, you don't have to draw the same shape as mine; there are many other shapes that you can chose.

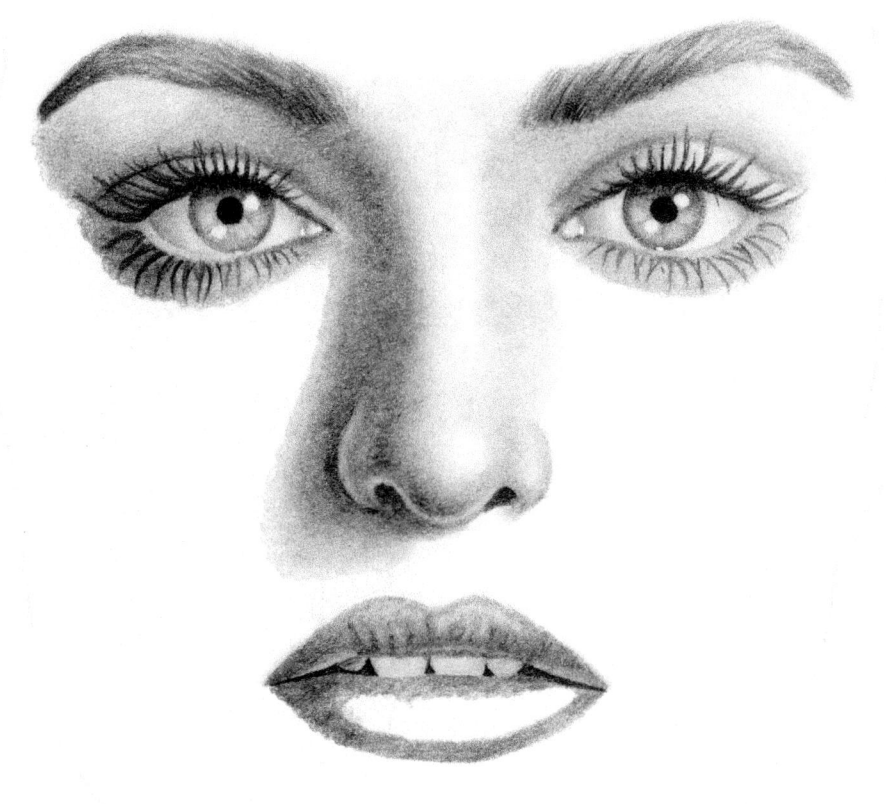

Now we can cover the mid area that we have left untouched with an HB. Don't press hard in the middle. Make a gradient transition between the basic tone of the lips and highlights by pressing harder next to the B areas, and releasing the pressure as you shade towards the highlights.

The lip should look round vertically and horizontally, that's why we should have the brightest highlight in the middle, and a less bright highlight all around it.

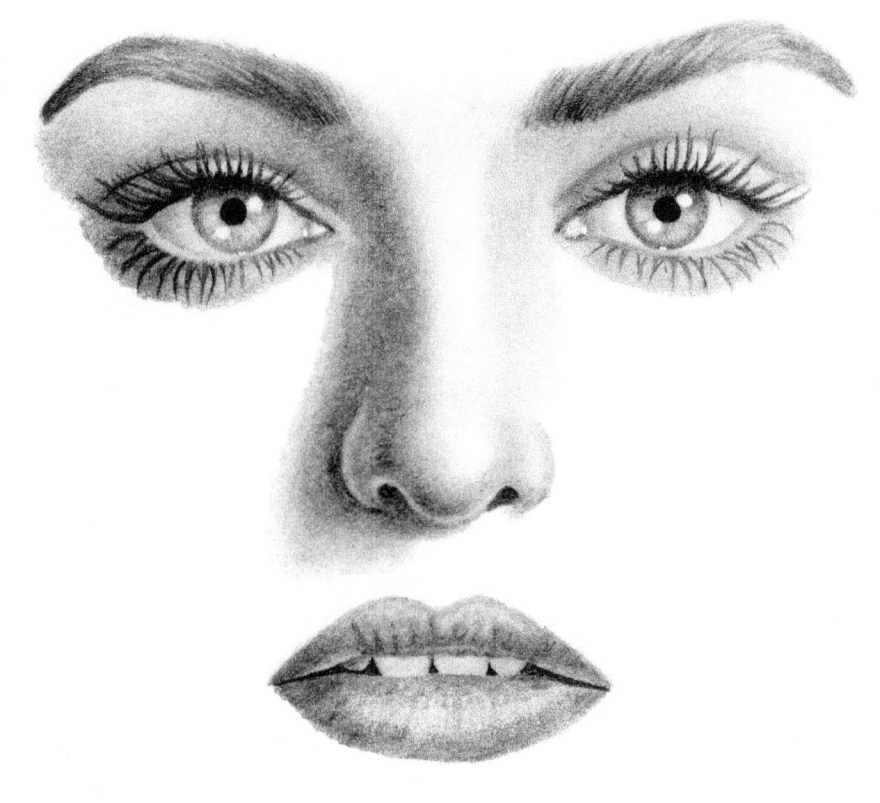

Blend it all with a Q-tip and you will see how smooth it will become. Use a blending stump for blending the edge or for blending smaller better details. If you remove very dark areas with blending, just draw over and strengthen the shadow again.

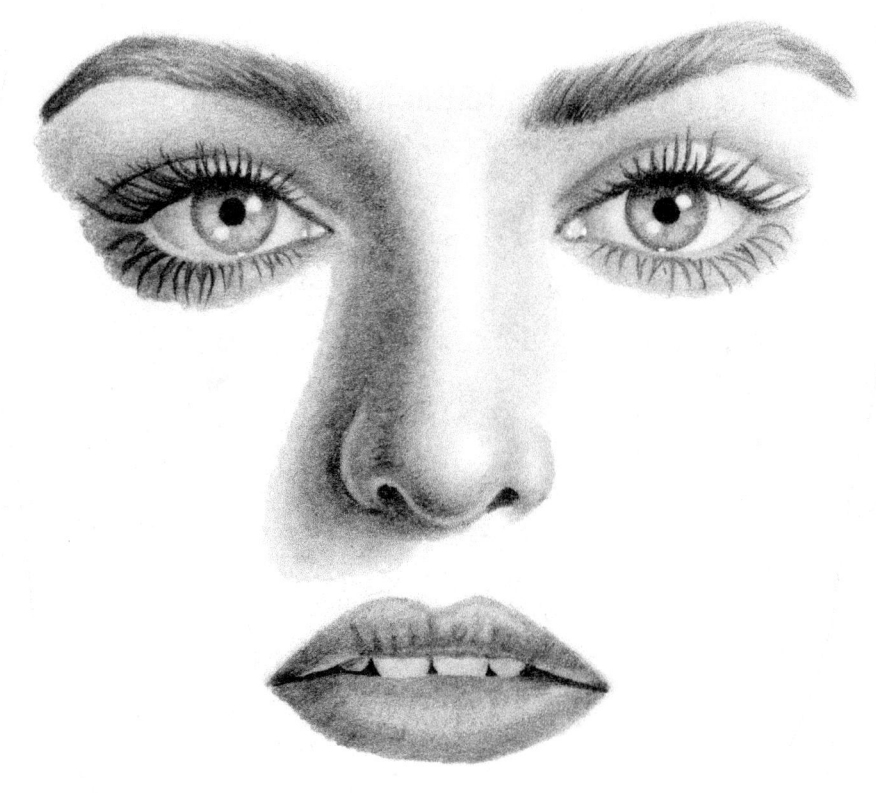

On upper lip, we have created the highlights first. Let's now create the shadows. Always try to approach drawing differently to gain more experience and learn to draw better. Strengthen the shadows that you created with a B pencil since they become brighter after blending. I'm using a B pencil again for this. Blend it a bit and create some wrinkles. Press harder over the shadowed areas on the left side. When shading under the teeth, leave out 1mm of the edge and shade under it. We need that brighter edge for the light reflected from the teeth. The brighter the reflected light, the glossier the lip will appear. So, you can create brighter or less bright reflected light, as you please; both would look good.

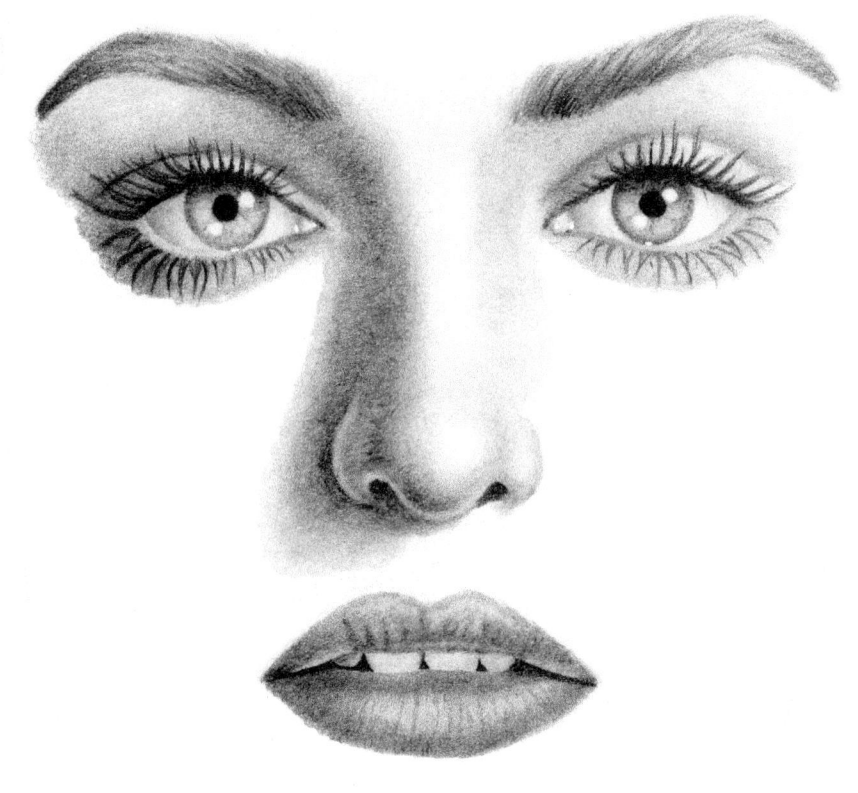

Now you can create the highlights over the lower lip. They should be the brightest in the very middle. Also, you can brighten up the light reflected from the teeth – as I did – and highlight the wrinkles too.

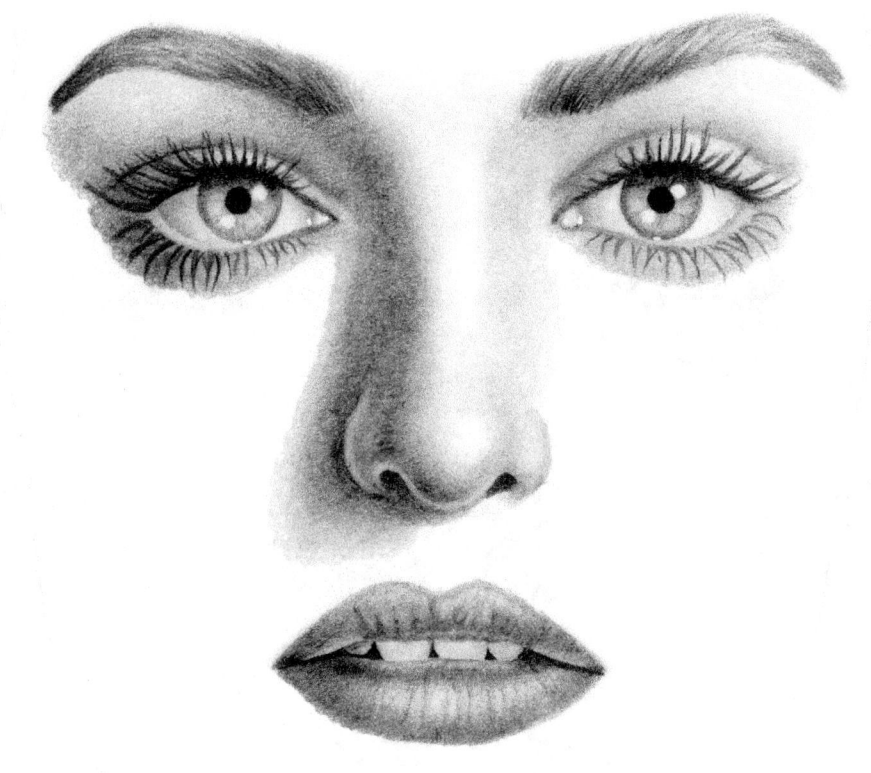

Shading the Skin

Now we can start shading the skin of the face. Let's focus only on a small area at a time and start with the darkest area on the left side, using an HB. Since we have already shaded the facial features as our light source is coming from the upper-right corner, we have to make the left side of the face much darker, maybe 1/3 of the width between the nose and ear, so left 1/3 should be covered in this step with an HB.

It is important to apply circulism technique all the time if you want to create a smooth texture of the human skin. You shouldn't use strokes or cross hatches for the skin. Circulism is drawing tiny, overlapping circles until you cover the paper. After that, you should blend it. For blending the larger areas, always use a tissue. For blending smaller areas, use a blending stump. Q-tips are good for blending mid-sized areas that are too small for a tissue and too big for a blending stump.

In the next image, you can see which areas I have shaded with an HB and that it still looks very rough. But don't worry, after blending it will look smooth.

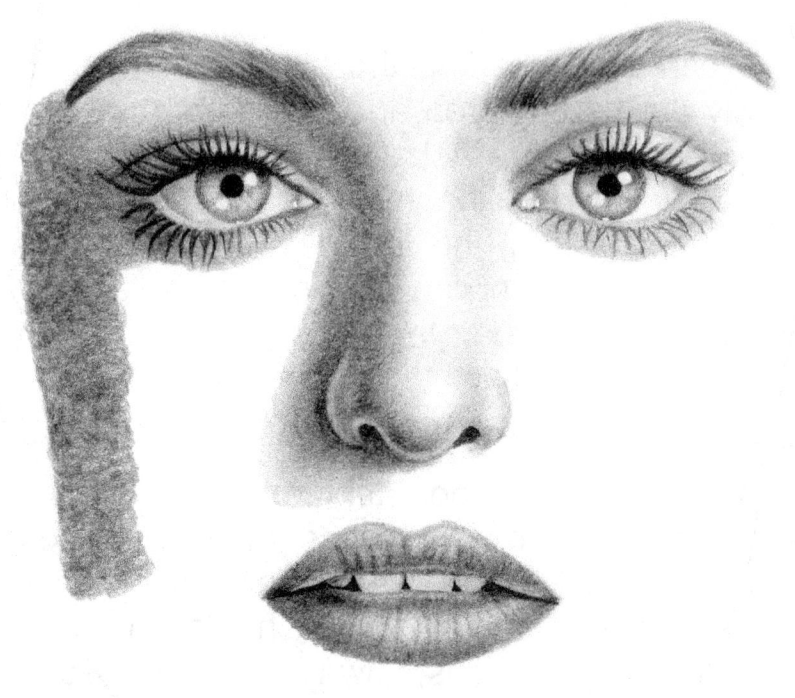

As a continuation to this, still using an HB, but pressing less, shade beside the right edge of the previously shaded area. Press less and less as you work towards the nose. Of course, use circular motions all the time. An HB is a very good pencil for this because you can achieve a really dark tone when you press hard, and much brighter as you relieve the pressure.

Shade larger area under the eye, just right above the cheek because this area gets shadow casted by the left eye.

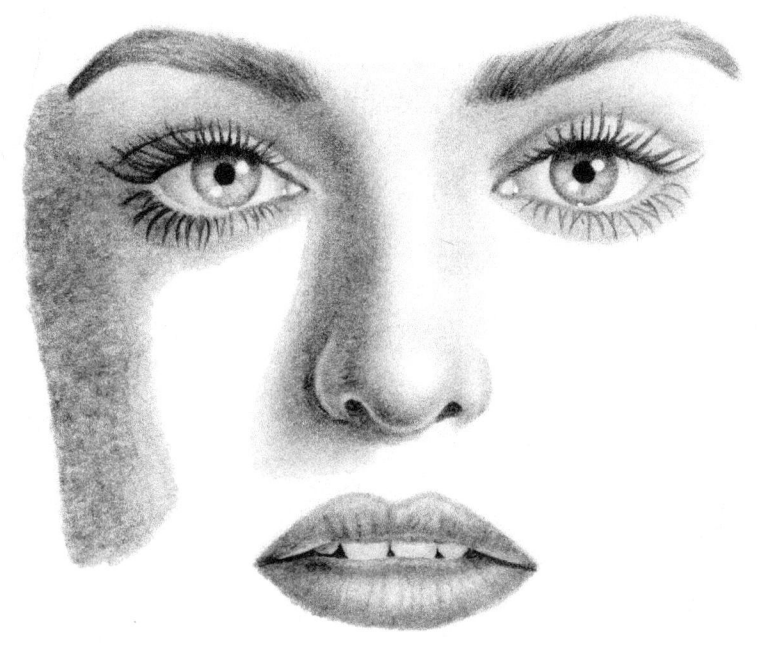

Now shade next to the previously shaded area and at the bottom of the cheek, as shown in the next image. Use a 2H for this area. Just connect the shadow cast by the nose with the one on the left side because this area under the cheek gets less light than the cheek itself.

Now you can see that the area that I left untouched for now is actually the highlight on this side of the face. You can start shading from highlights next time, to try out different methods and see which one can bring better results. Also, shade a bit next to the nose, about 1-2 mm thick edge add to the shaded part of the left side of the nose. So, basically, all around the brightest highlight should be left untouched.

If you see some imperfections or that the edge between the tones is visible, don't worry. We are going to blend it and to do some finishing touches to refine the texture if necessary.

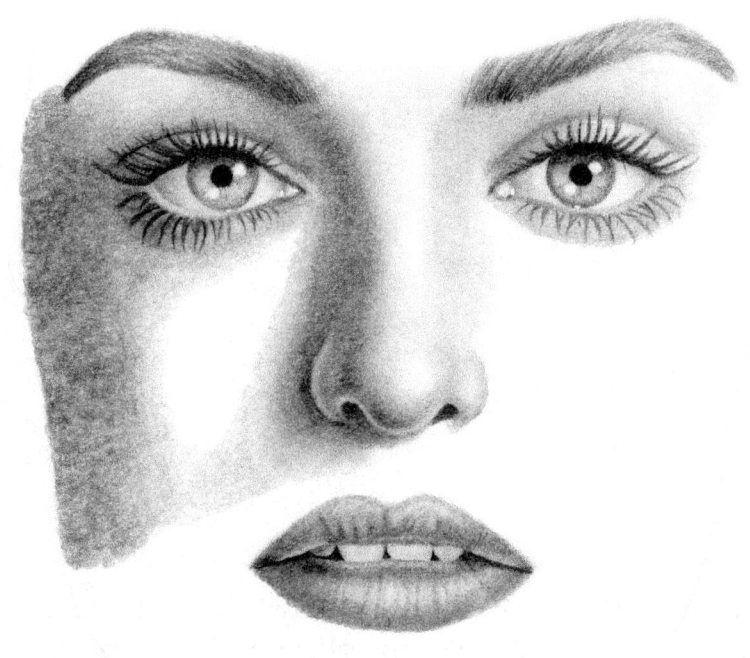

Now we can fill the rest of this area with a 6H. I have a 6H, but you can use 7h or 5H, if you have these. Press a bit more next to the edge of the previously shaded area and release the pressure as you shade towards the center of the highlight because, as always, gradient transition is very important. The highlight should look much brighter, yet it shouldn't stay white.

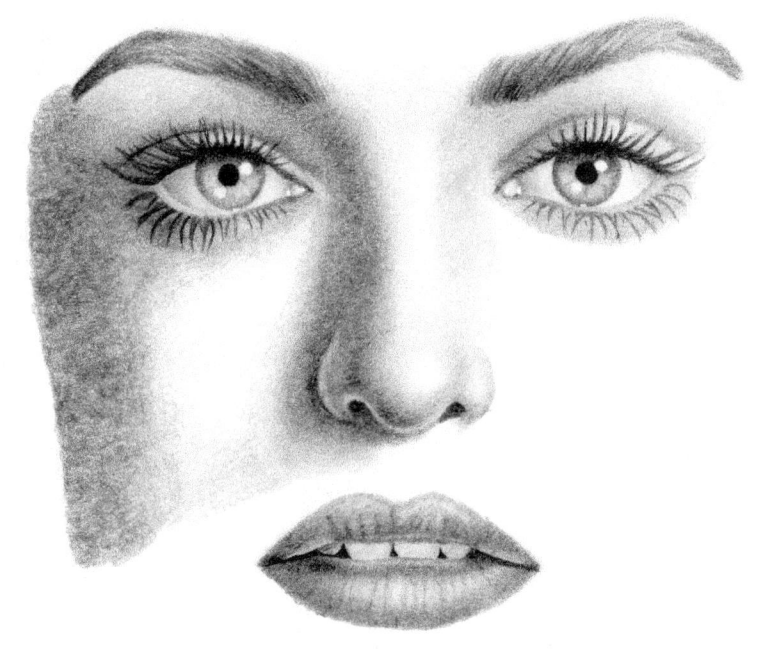

Now blend it all with a tissue. If you start over the darkest part, do not shade with that part of the tissue over the highlight. Start from the highlight, using circular motions with a tissue wrapped around your finger and blend towards the dark shadow. This way you wont darken the highlights.

In the next image, you can see how smooth the texture looks after blending. There is a huge difference in the before and after.

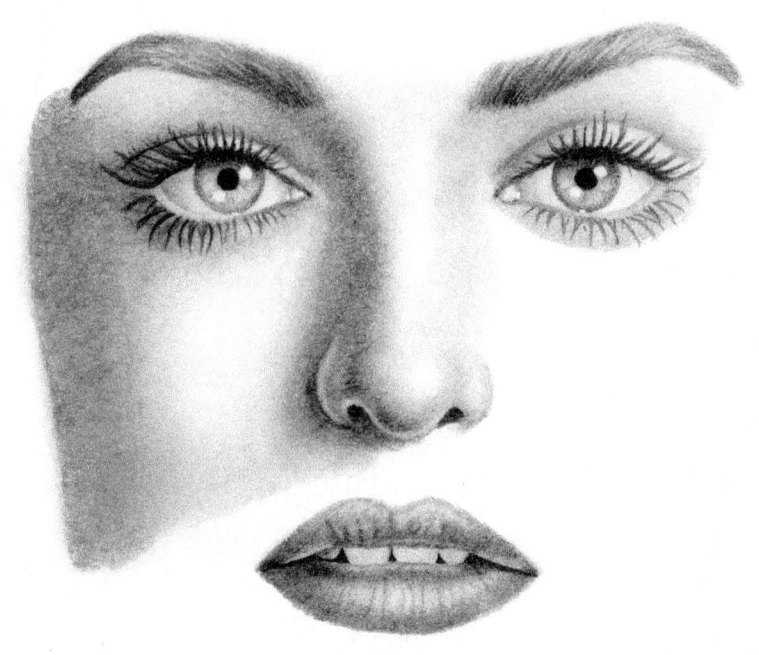

You can add some shades if you have brightened them up. You can even use some darker pencil, such as B, to strengthen the shadow under the eye and on the very left side, next to the ear. As I mentioned, some imperfections are just quite good such as moles, tiny wrinkles, or hairs.

Now we can move to the forehead. Place a clean piece of paper over the eyes and other drawn areas so that you don't smudge it.

As you know, the forehead is round and we have to create a gradient transition from shadows to highlights. Start on the left side, using an HB, pressing more on the very left side, next to the hair and around the eyebrow. Release the pressure as you shade in circular motions towards the highlight. Highlight would be found above the right eyebrow, almost in the center of the forehead. Shade the area shown in the next image.

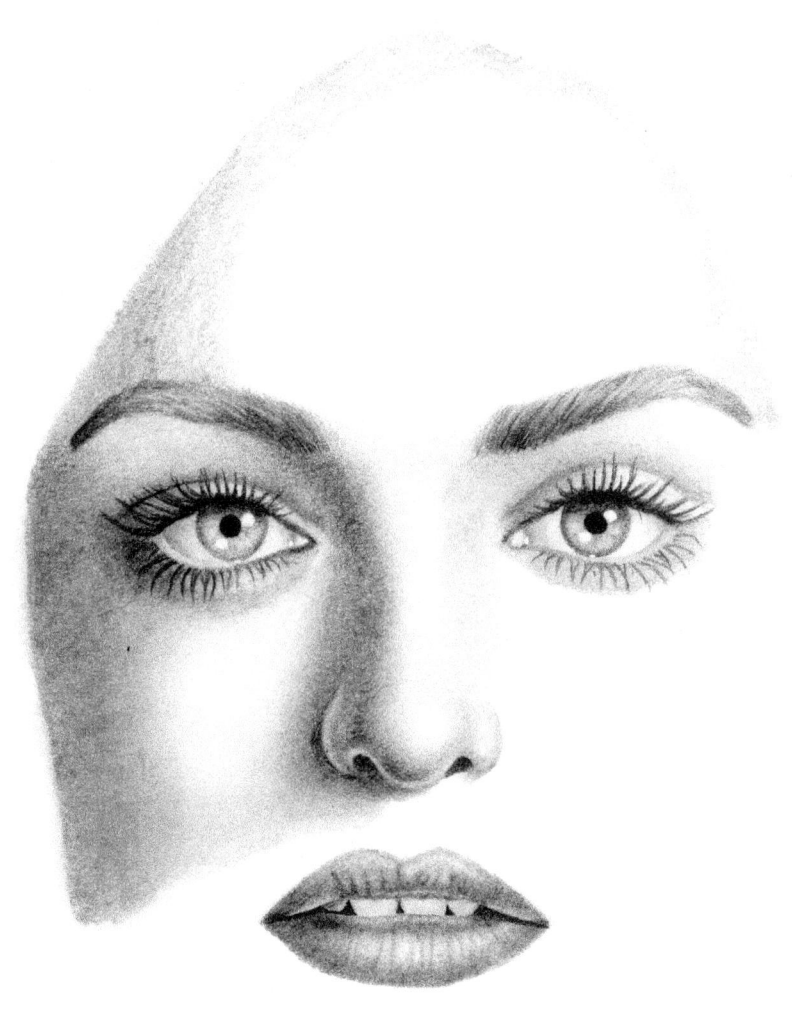

Now you can shade the rest of the forehead, except for the highlight. Since it is very difficult to explain with words, I have divided the areas with digital lines in the next image, so that you can better understand which area to shade in this step.

I have marked the area for the highlight, which should stay untouched because the light source in the upper-right corner would create a very strong, white highlight over this part of the forehead. You can see also that I have written "highlight" over the eyebrow and the skin above it, which we were shading according to this. So, basically, this is the same highlight, we just have an eyebrow over it.

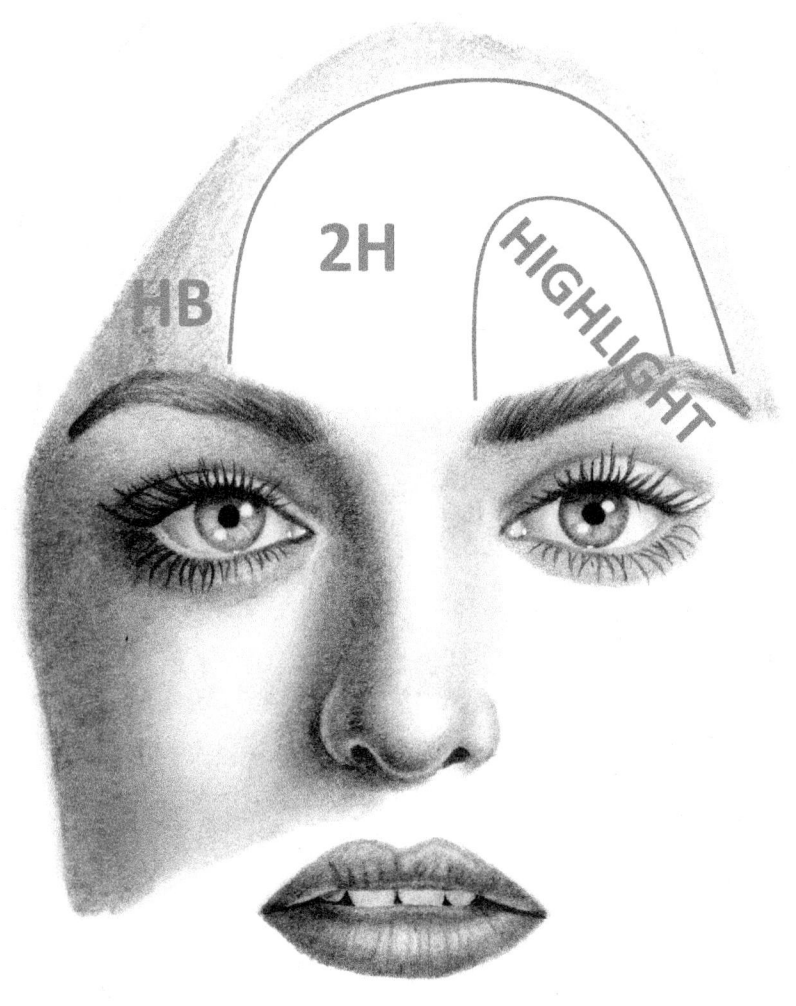

Shade this whole area with a 2H, pressing lightly, and of course, press less as you shade around the highlight. In the next image you can see how my area looks pretty pale, but we are going to blend it with a tissue and as you may notice when you blend yourself, the area becomes darker. Not to mention that the scanner makes the images I photocopy very bright, so my drawing is always actually a bit darker.

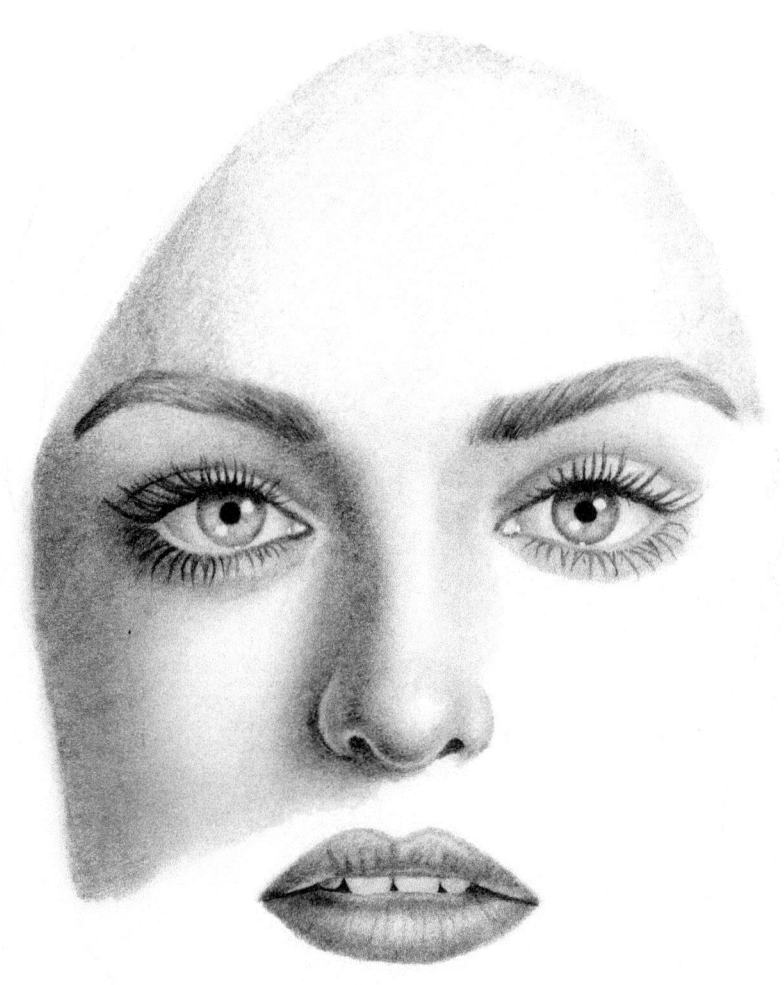

Now blend it all with a tissue. Press harder in a circular motion all around the forehead, making sure to skip the highlight; do not go over the eyebrows.

Now you can see how it becomes quite dark, yet it is not too dark. Add more shade between the eyebrows with a 2H, if necessary, and blend it again. This area is a bit bent inwards usually, of course not on every person, but usually always at least a little self-shadow is there. This way we can make the frontal bone even more protruding, so that we show that the forehead is a bit closer to the viewers eyes than the nose bridge base.

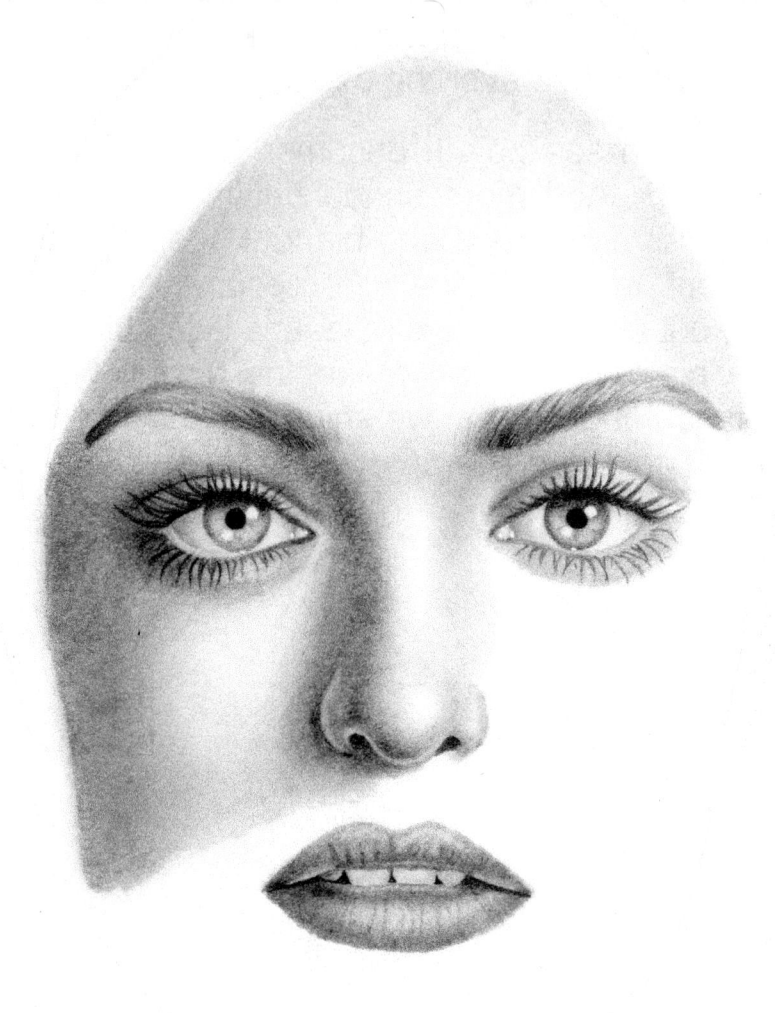

Let's move to the right side of the face. Here we have to use brighter tones, and more areas have to stay white. Start with a 2H and shade the temple, press less next to the highlights. Now, here is the question whether we want to draw the ear or just a hair. Actually I want to draw the ear to show you how to draw and shade it, but we can cover it later with hair, for example. But, if we have the hair next to the face, the right edge of the face will be quite shadowed, so we have to determine now, or maybe to improve later. It is easier to add it later than to erase, so if we have the hair here we can just shade more. So, let's shade normally for now.

After shading the temple, continue downwards and shade the right side of the face in the same manner - a 2H, circular motions. About 1/3 of this width between the nose and the ear. As I mentioned already, use the dull tip of the pencil so that you won't scratch the paper and you can actually cover a larger area with a dull tip and progress faster than when you have a very sharp point.

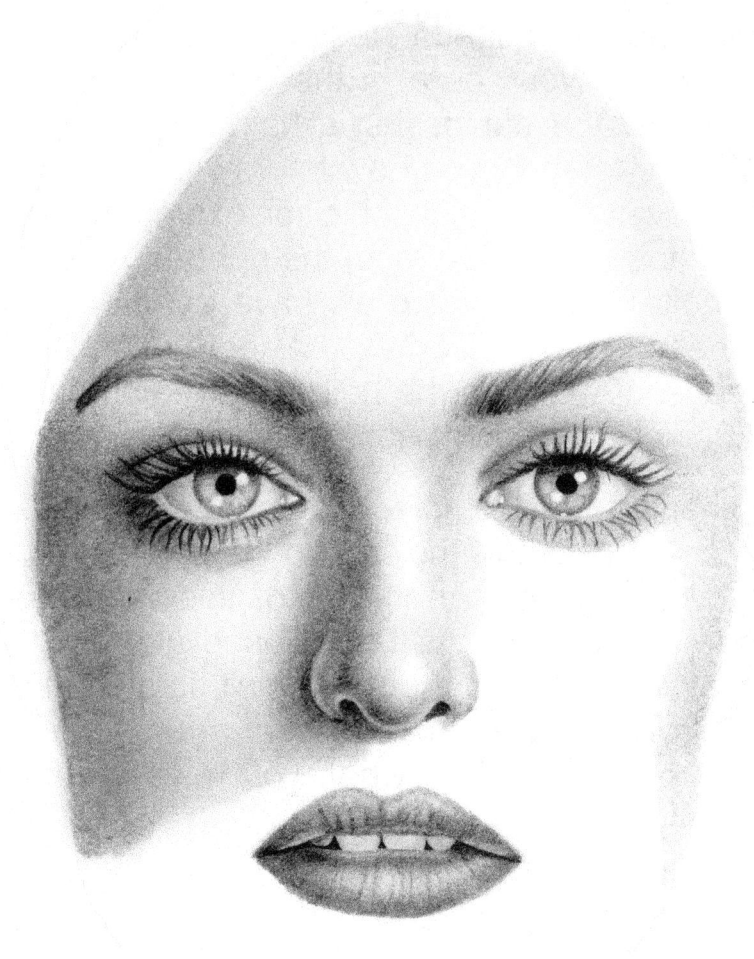

Next, move to the area next to it: the cheek and under the right eye. Use a 6H for this area because it should be very bright.

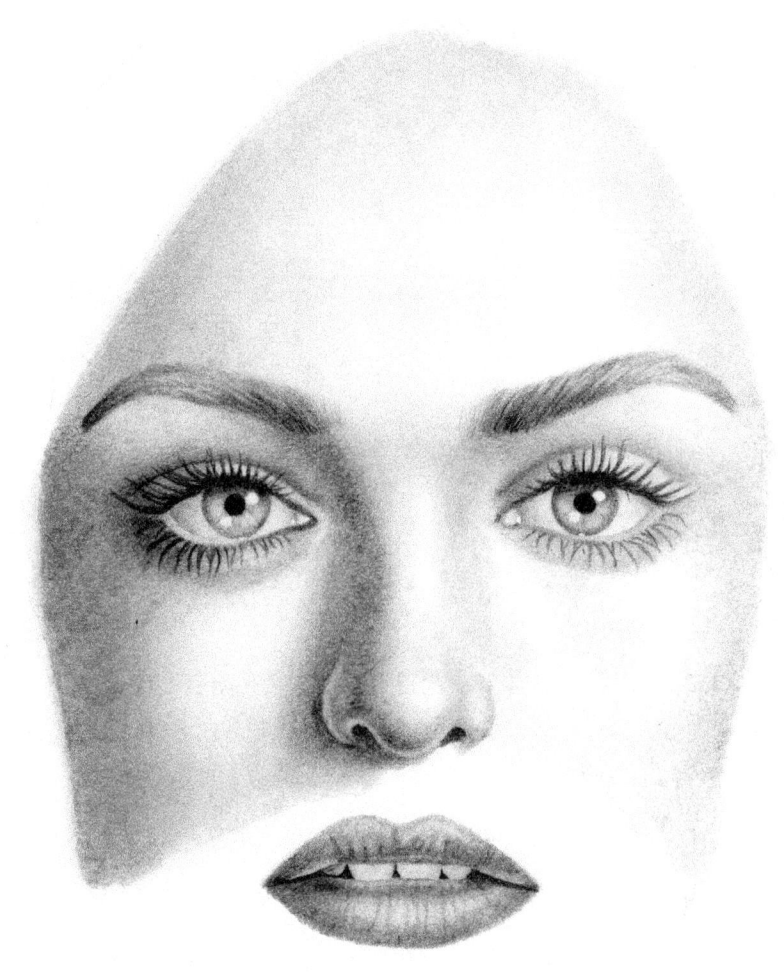

Now you can blend it all with a tissue, starting from very bright tones towards the ear. Always use a clean piece of a tissue, the one that you haven't used for blending before, so that you won't apply graphite from it over the highlights.

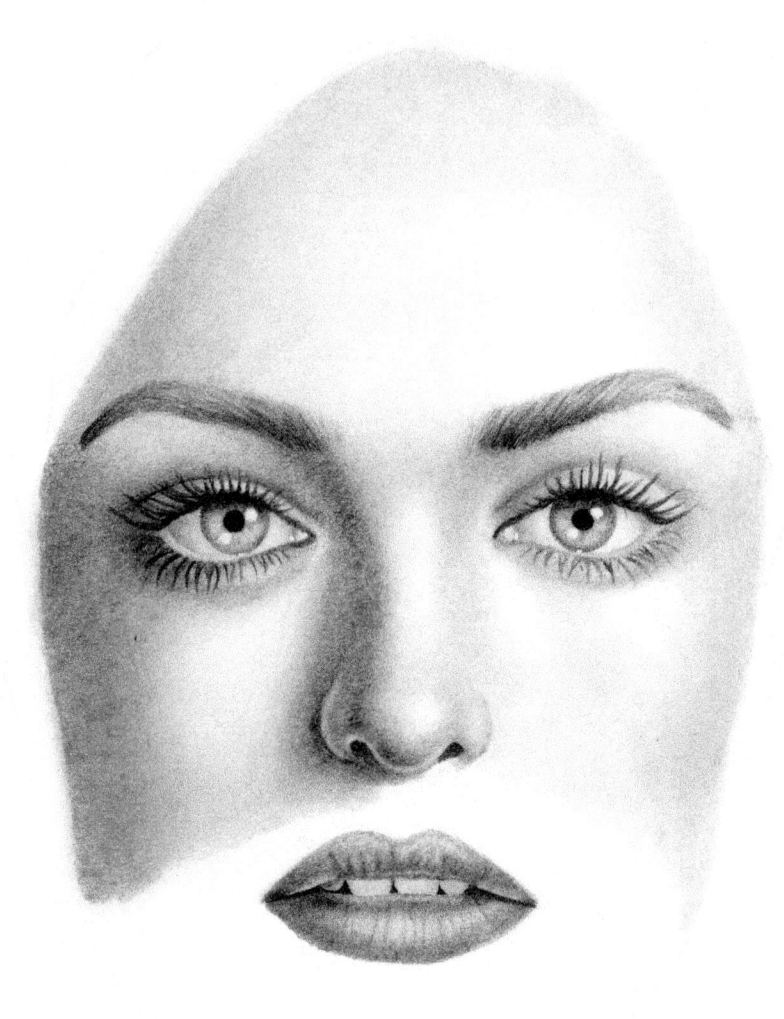

Let's divide the rest of the face into two phases: shading around the mouth and shading the chin.

First, shade the skin above the right side of the upper lip and connect it with the shadow cast by the nose that you shaded before. Use an HB here, and also shade the right side of this sag above the Cupid's bow, using medium pressure and going over the area again and again, if necessary.

Continue shading the left side of the face where you stopped before you moved to the forehead. Between this shaded area and the lips we have a bit of a brighter part that gets more light, so skip it for now and shade around the left corner of the lips. Study the next image carefully before you start to shade.

Keep applying circular motions all the time.

To help you better understand which areas I have shaded in this step, I have outlined them with digital lines that you can see in the next image.

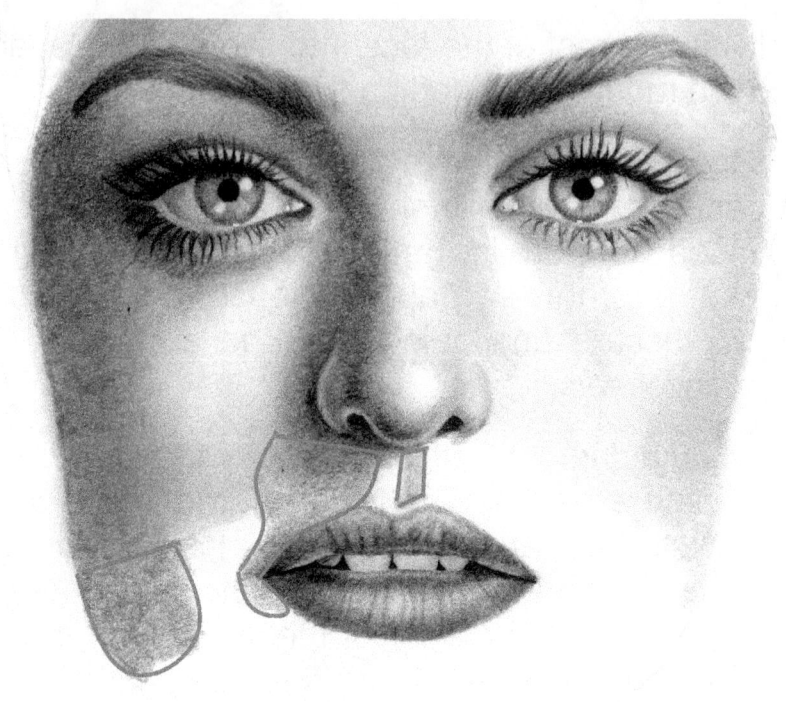

Here you can see how they look without digital lines. So, I used an HB for all these parts.

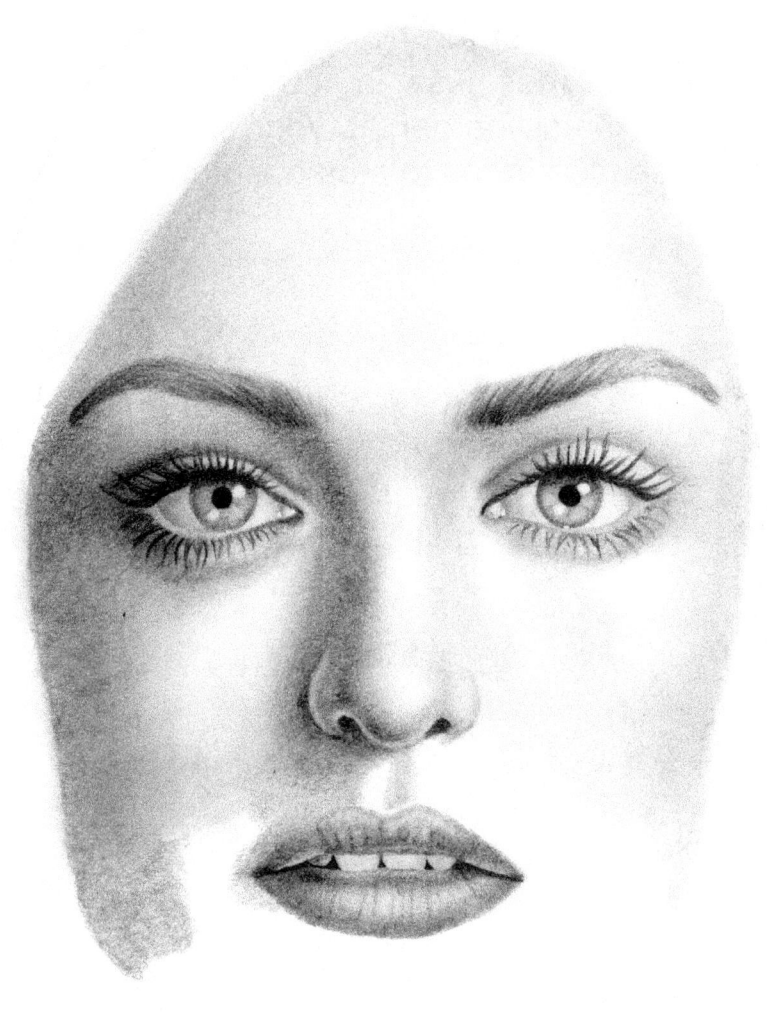

Now we can shade the rest of this area with a 2H. This is the area that we left untouched in the previous step. This highlight is much brighter than the surrounding areas, but still much darker than the highlight under the left eye, which is also much darker than the highlight under the right eye. So, there should be a difference between the tones of the highlights; the same goes for the shadows. Press less in the very middle of this highlight and press harder as your shade towards the previously shaded areas to create a gradual transition.

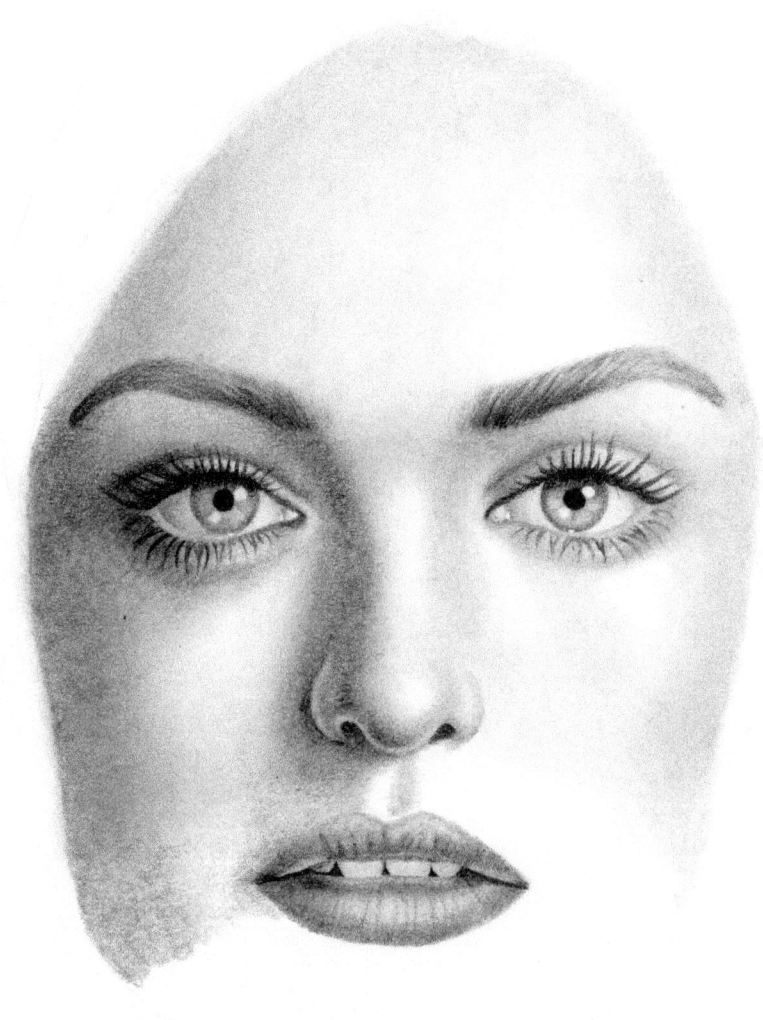

Blend this all with a tissue, starting over the highlights, using circular motion. After blending, you can see whether you need to add more shade or not.

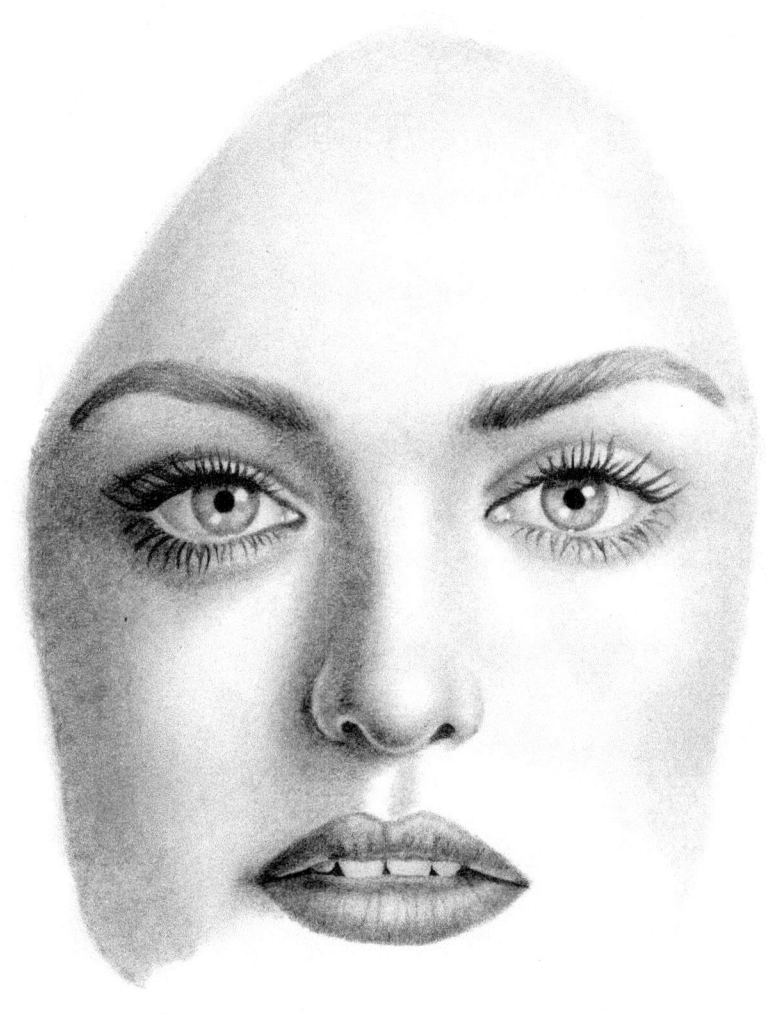

Now we can continue on the right side, above the lips and the whole area around the right corner of the lips. Shade everything in circular motion using a 6H and don't press too hard. Keep the same pressure to create the same tone everywhere. Blend it all with a tissue.

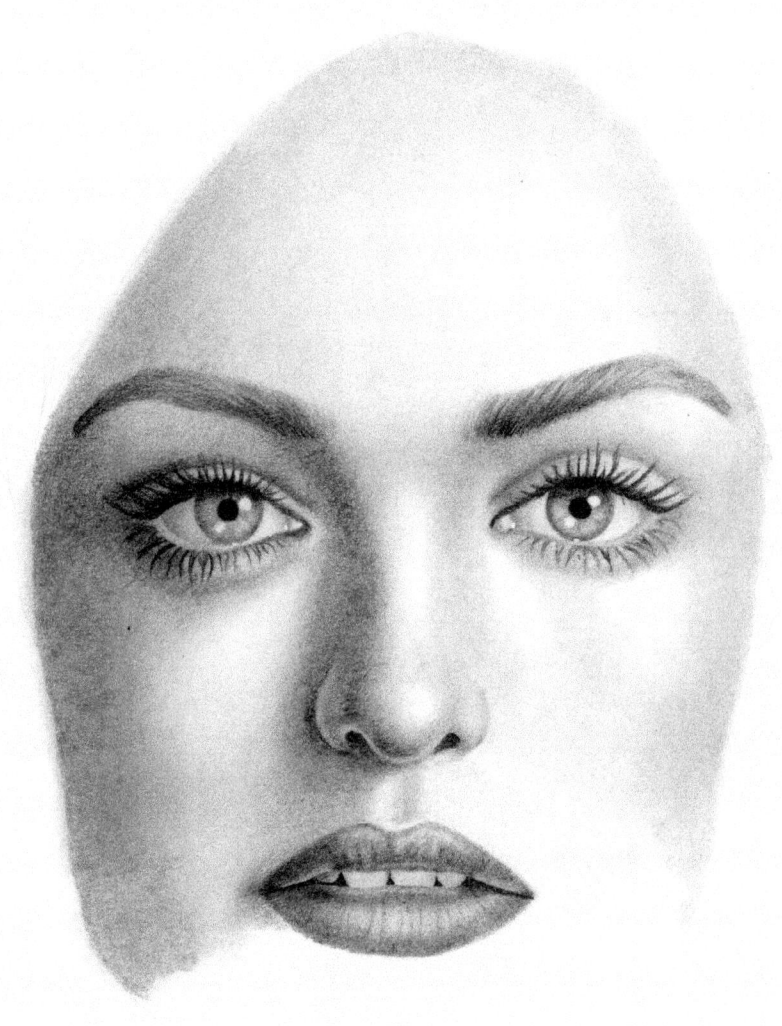

Now we can continue on the right side of the face that we shaded with 2H while also using circular motions. Press harder on the very right side and release the pressure as you shade towards the mouth. This way you are creating the roundness of the head, or actually of the face, by shading more on the right sides and less in the middle.

We can leave the chin for the latest phase of this drawing. So, focus on a tiny area at a time. Little by little, it will become a whole picture. Shade the right corner of the lips by pressing hard next to the lips and make this shading disappear into the surrounding tone.

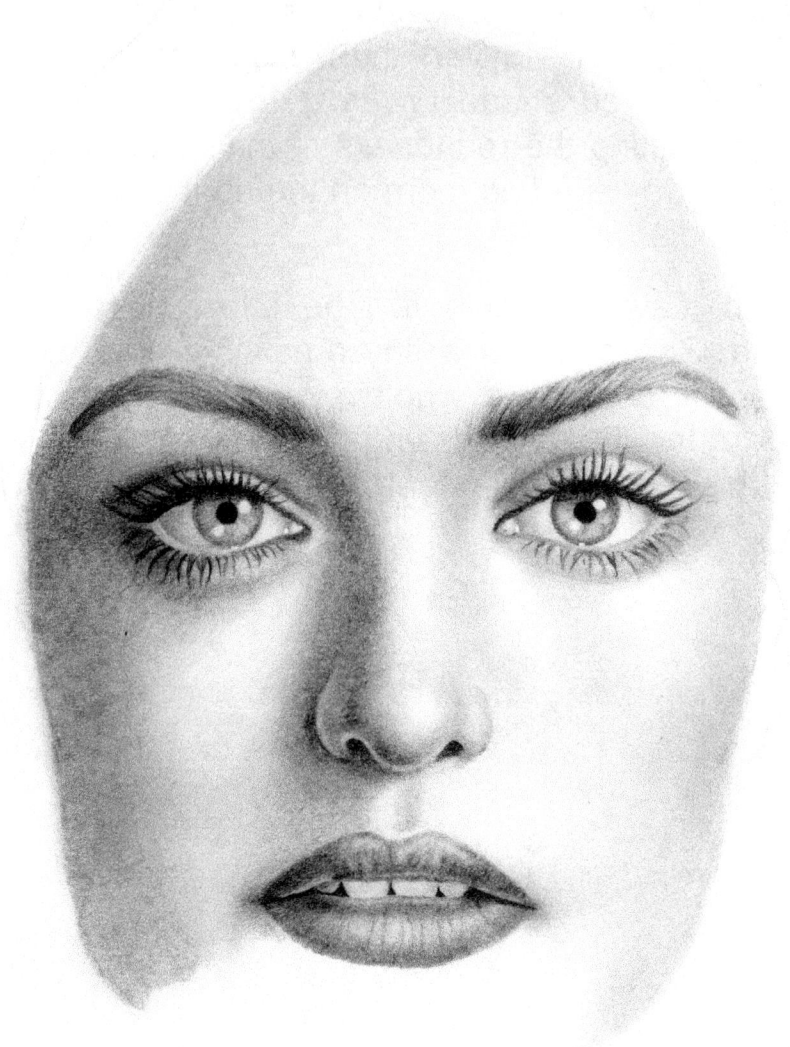

Let's finish the face by shading the rest of the lower area. Using an HB pencil, start shading the cast shadow under the lower lip, pressing harder, and continue towards the left side of the chin. Also, shade the edge of the jaw, still using an HB in circular motions.

An HB is pretty dark for this area, and we have to leave out the area in the middle of the chin, which gets a lot of light.

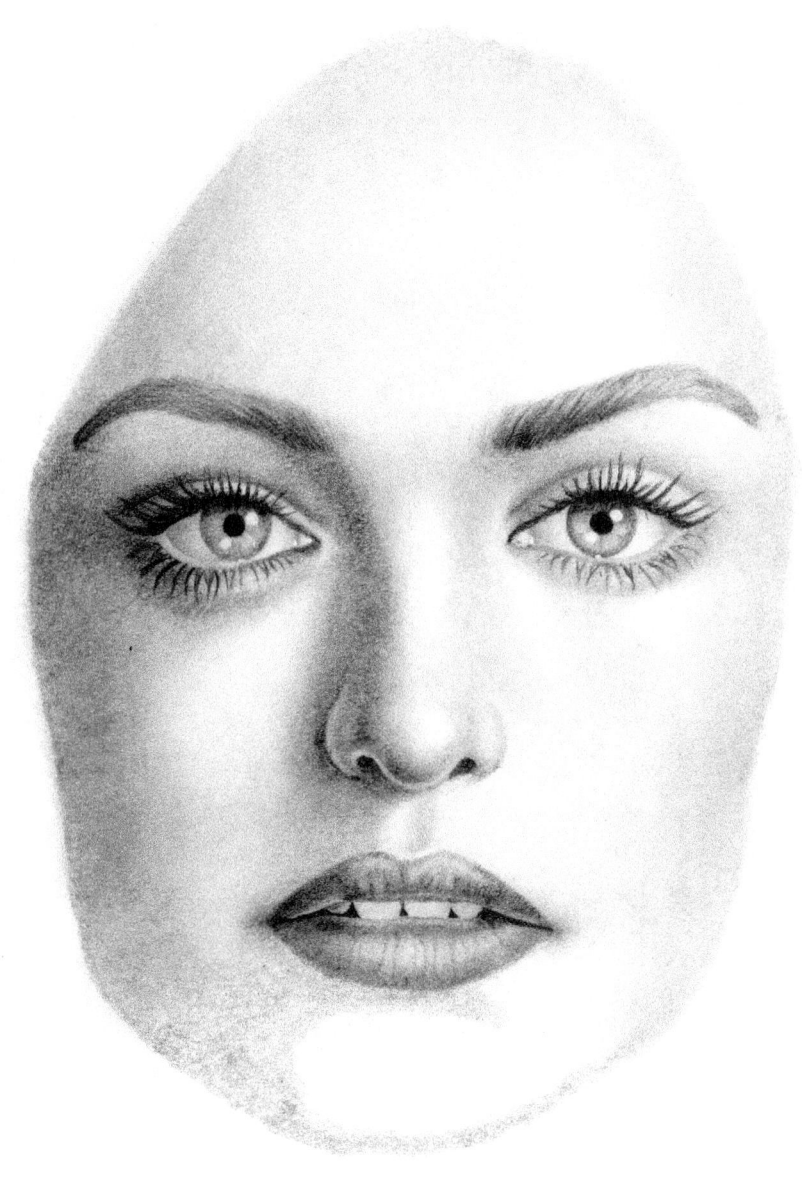

Shade the parts between the highlights and the previously shaded area. Basically, just leave out the middle of the chin untouched and shade around it with a 3H. As always, press harder next to the HB area and release the pressure as you shade towards the highlights. Also, shade the rest of the bottom-right part of the face, using this very bright tone, a 3H, dull point.

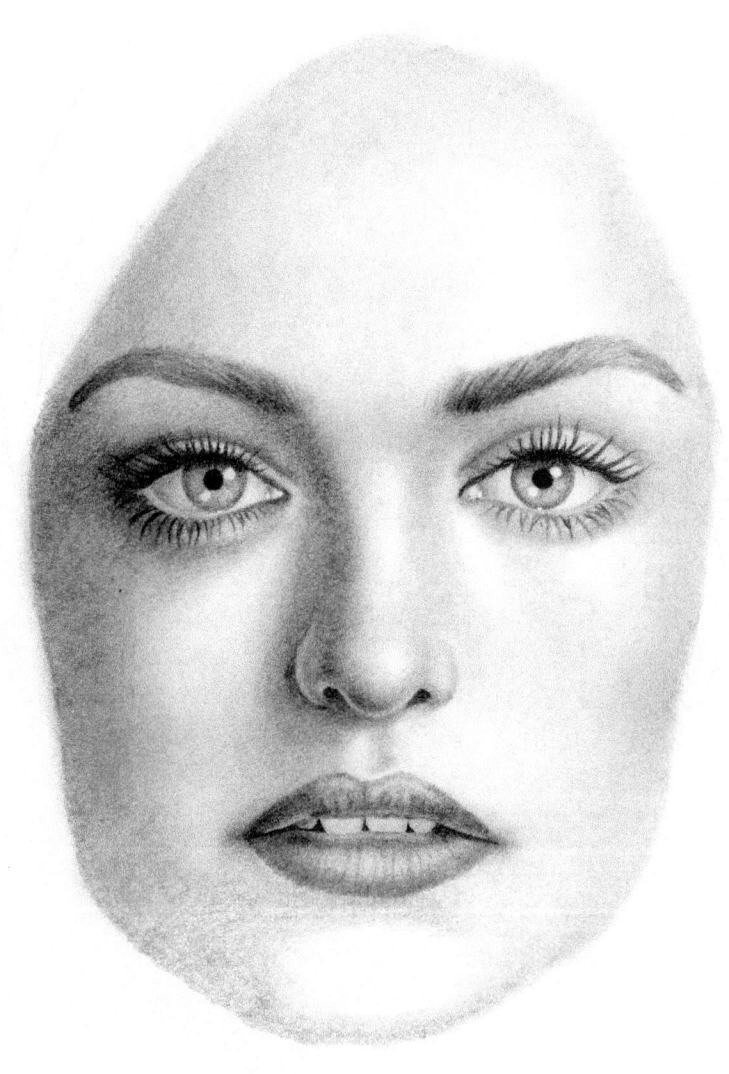

Use a 6H to shade a bit more around the highlights to make the gradient transition better.

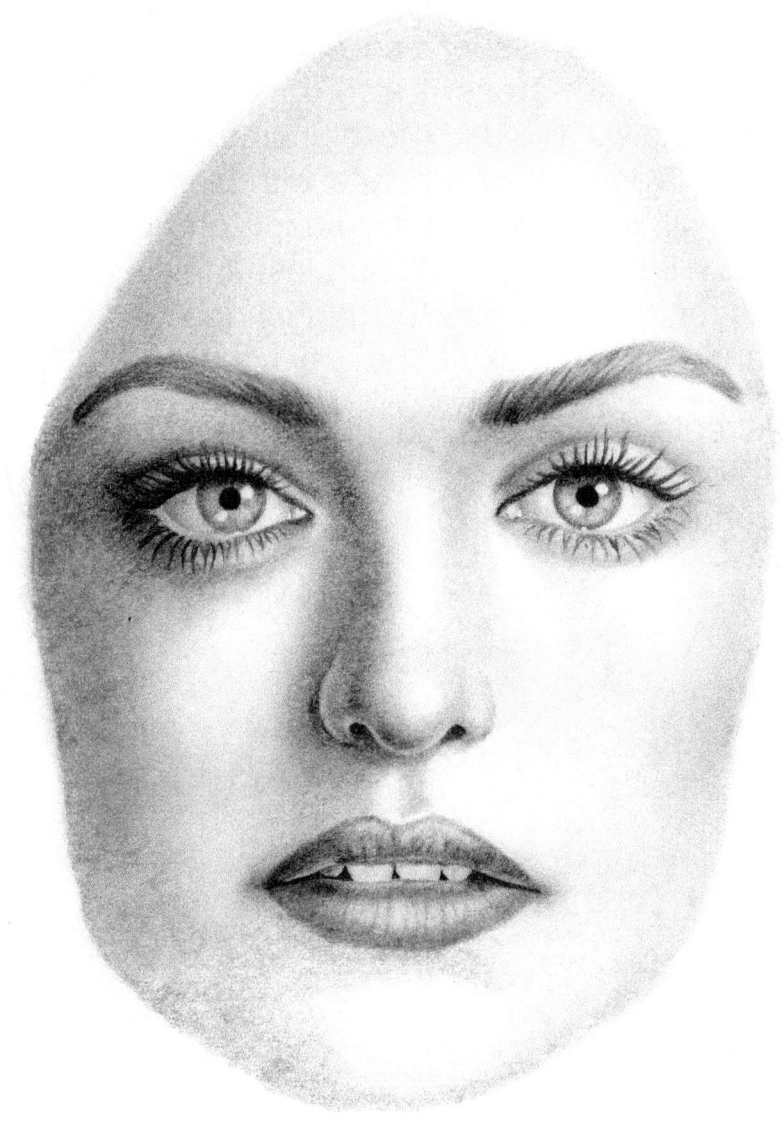

Blend this all with a tissue. I have shaded a bit over the area for the neck as I shaded the edge, but it doesn't matter because we are going to shade it next.

Start blending over the highlighted area first. Using a clean piece of a tissue, use circular motions to blend towards the dark areas. I also darkened a bit the area under the lower lip, using a blending stump because I have removed a lot of graphite with blending. This cast shadow will also suggest the shape of the lip and how full it is. If it is darker, it will suggest a fullness of the lip; the bigger the shadow, the bigger the lip. So, it's all arbitrary. You can make it the way you want.

Also, create a reflected light under the lip by erasing the lower edge with an eraser. This will add even more to the roundness of the lip.

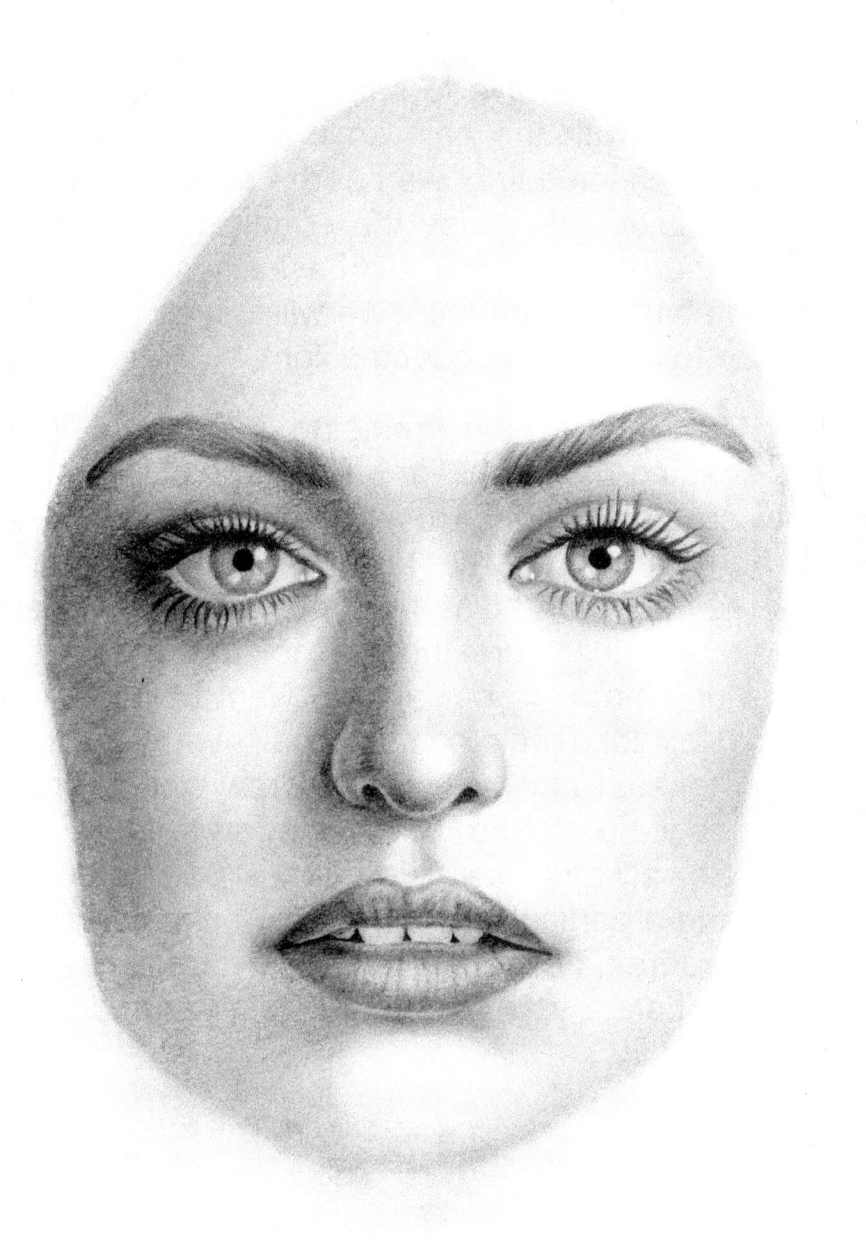

We are not done with the face yet. The only thing left is to create the reflected light over the edge of the chin. But before that, we have to shade the part of the neck which borders with the chin so that we can see how bright is the reflected light we need. For now, it wouldn't be quite visible if we erase the edge and we wouldn't know whether it is enough. So basically, we're starting working on the neck and then we will just go back to the face again to create the reflected light.

Take a look at the next image to see where I have started shading the neck. I'm using an 8B to create the shadow cast by the face over the neck, and using a very dark pencil for the area next to the chin. As always, as you work away from the face, just create a brighter tone. Now here the tone of the shadow also depends on what kind of hair you want to draw. If you want to draw long hair or black hair, you should use very dark tones. But if you want to draw blonde or short hair, you should use a B for the area that I have shaded. So, always use a few tones brighter nuance than I use in a particular step. But, you shouldn't try out as a new portrait. For now, it is best if you follow and do the same. Later, you can experiment and do many things differently.

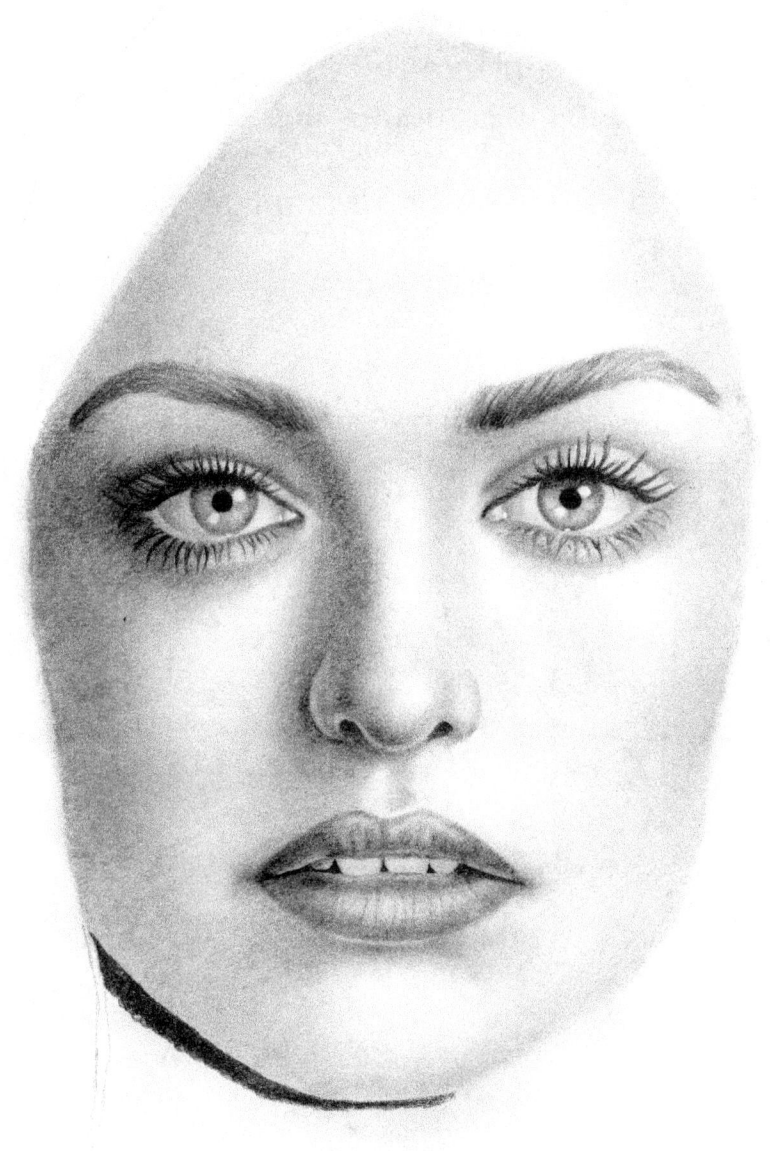

As a continuation to this 8B area, use a B next to it, press harder over the 8B area, and press less as you work away from the face. Here also, make sure you are applying the Circulism method the entire time. Since our light source is coming from the upper-right corner, it will cast a very strong and huge shadow in the upper-left corner of the neck. Just imagine the shape of the chin, or take a look in the mirror, but place the light source to upper-right area of your face and see what kind of shape of the shadow the chin will cast. If it seems to be too dark, we're going to blend it with a tissue and to remove a bit of graphite, so just use the dark tones confidently.

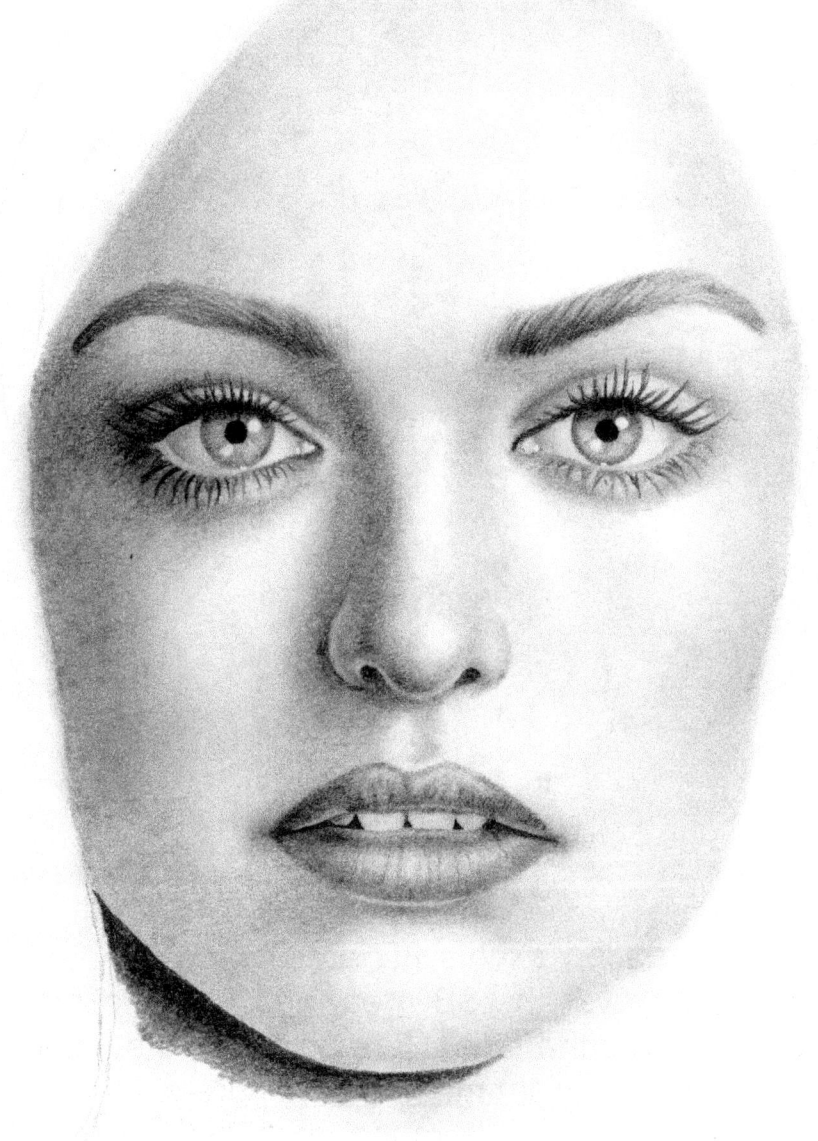

Now that we have created a bordering part of this cast shadow, we can go back to the face to create a reflected light. But you don't have to actually erase the edge for the reflected light because it's pretty bright, maybe even too bright. So, using an HB, shade the area of the chin but leave out the edge, about 1mm or so, and shade next to this edge. Of course, you can even erase a bit of the edge if you want. It would suggest a very glossy skin, but you can try it anyway. If it's too bright, you just cover it with graphite again. Don't be afraid of using dark tones; you can make any mistake because you practice this way and gain experience. The dark tones will add depth to your drawing.

As you draw towards the center of the face, press less and less to create that gradient transition. You can see after I have shaded this area the edge became brighter, though I haven't brightened the reflected light. This is how we enhance the brightness, by shading around it. Now the chin appears much rounder and more 3-D.

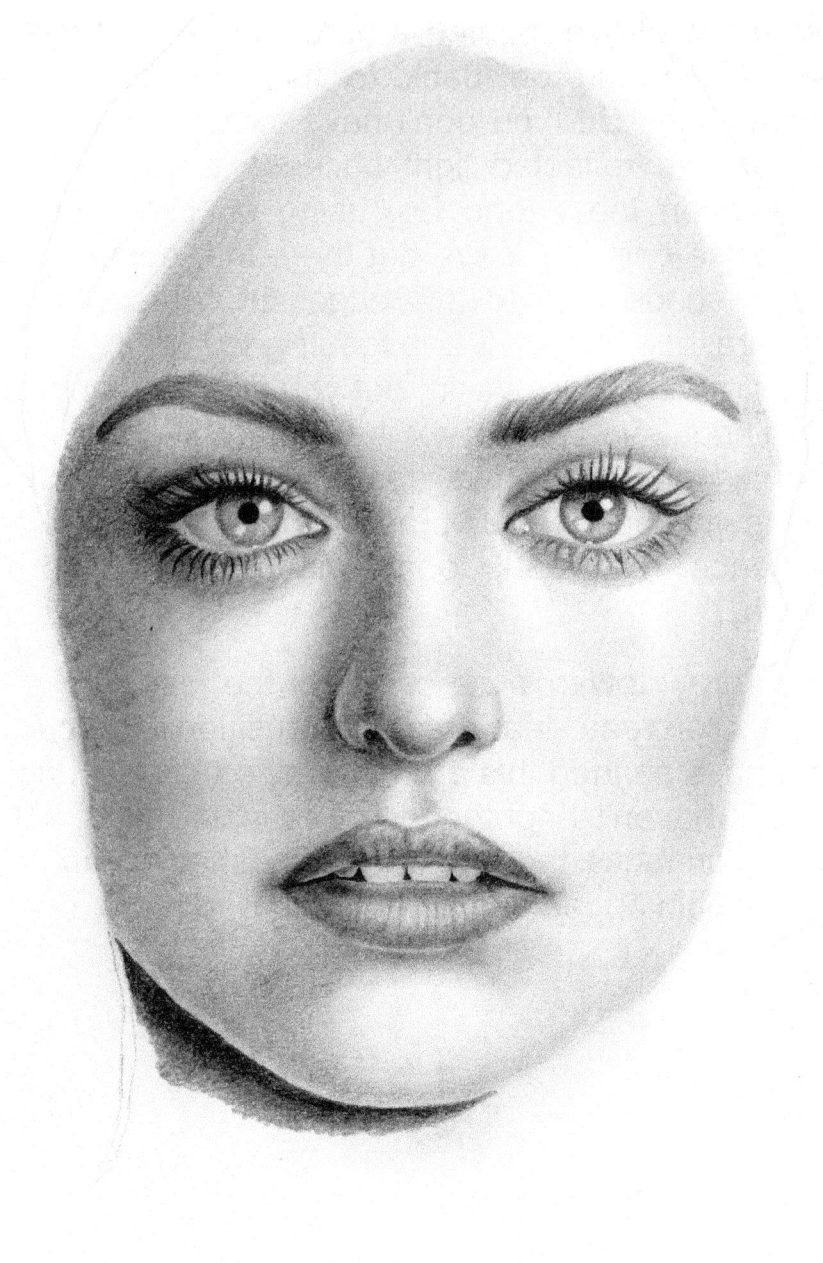

We're not going to draw much of the neck because we want to focus on the face in this tutorial, but as you see, the upper part of the neck is important to draw too because of this cast shadow. So, let's finish shading a bit of the neck under this cast shadow and on the right , brighter side as well.

Using an HB continue drawing the cast shadow under the area shaded with a B where we stopped before we moved back to the face. Now shade a bit of a larger area as shown in the next image and also continue shading under the chin on the right side. We have to have a shadow on the right side too, but not as dark and large as on the left side, so an HB is just enough, as long as you don't press too hard. You should create this part tick, and slowly increase its size as you shade towards the mid area. This will suggest that the top of the chin is found quite further from the neck than the right side of the corners of the chin. Here also, apply circular motions and press harder next for to the face, right under the face, and release the pressure as you shade downwards. On the right side we should now have a very tiny and bright shadow cast, and on the left side a very dark and big shadow cast. If you want to draw a male portrait, think of the Adam's apple, it would cast the shadow too. We're going to blend it all, but before that, we have to create bright areas as well.

You can see now how the face actually seems to be closer to our eyes due to the shadow cast over the neck.

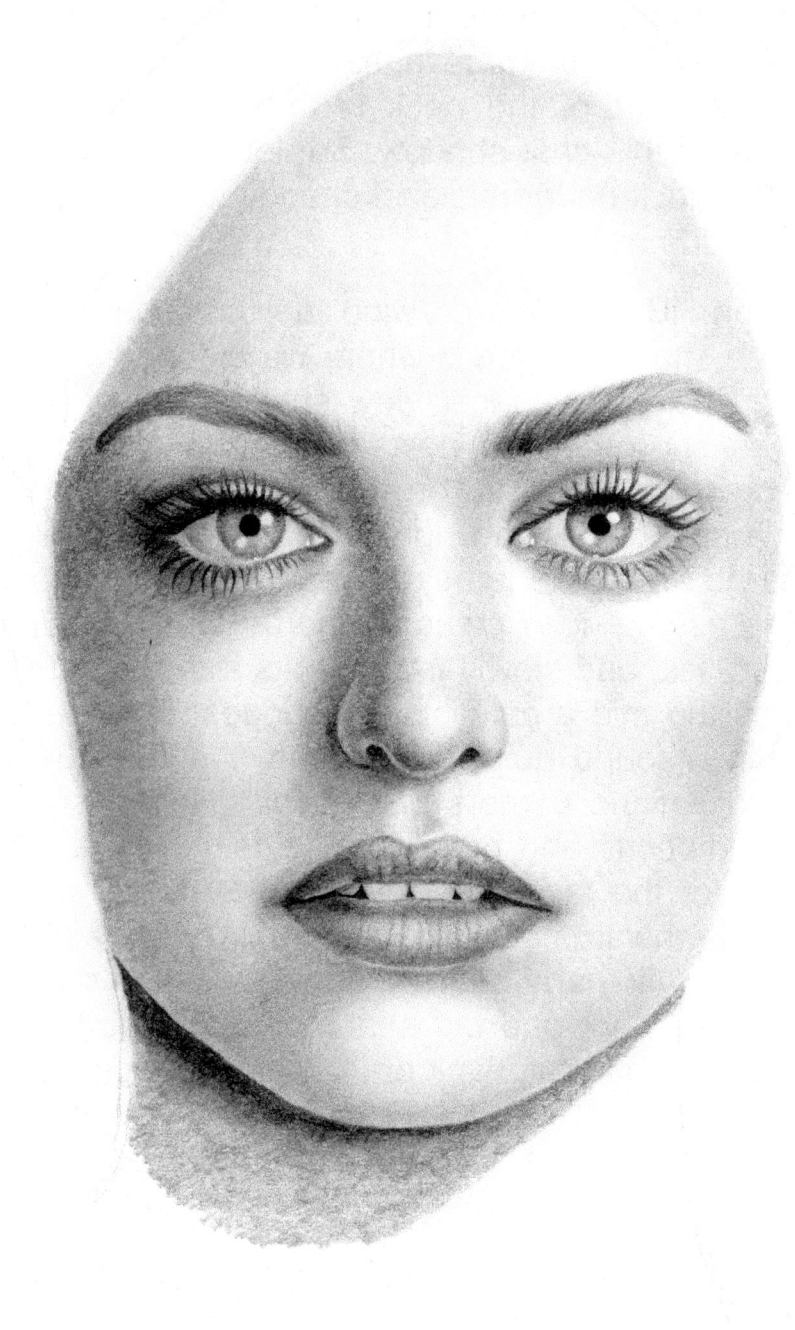

Using a 2H pencil, shade under the HB areas. Press very hard next to it and then as you work away from it, press less and less. That gradient transition is important here too. Shade the edge of the neck on the left side and, as always, press harder next to the edge. This will make the neck appear round.

In the next image you can see which area I left untouched. This area should be the brightest.

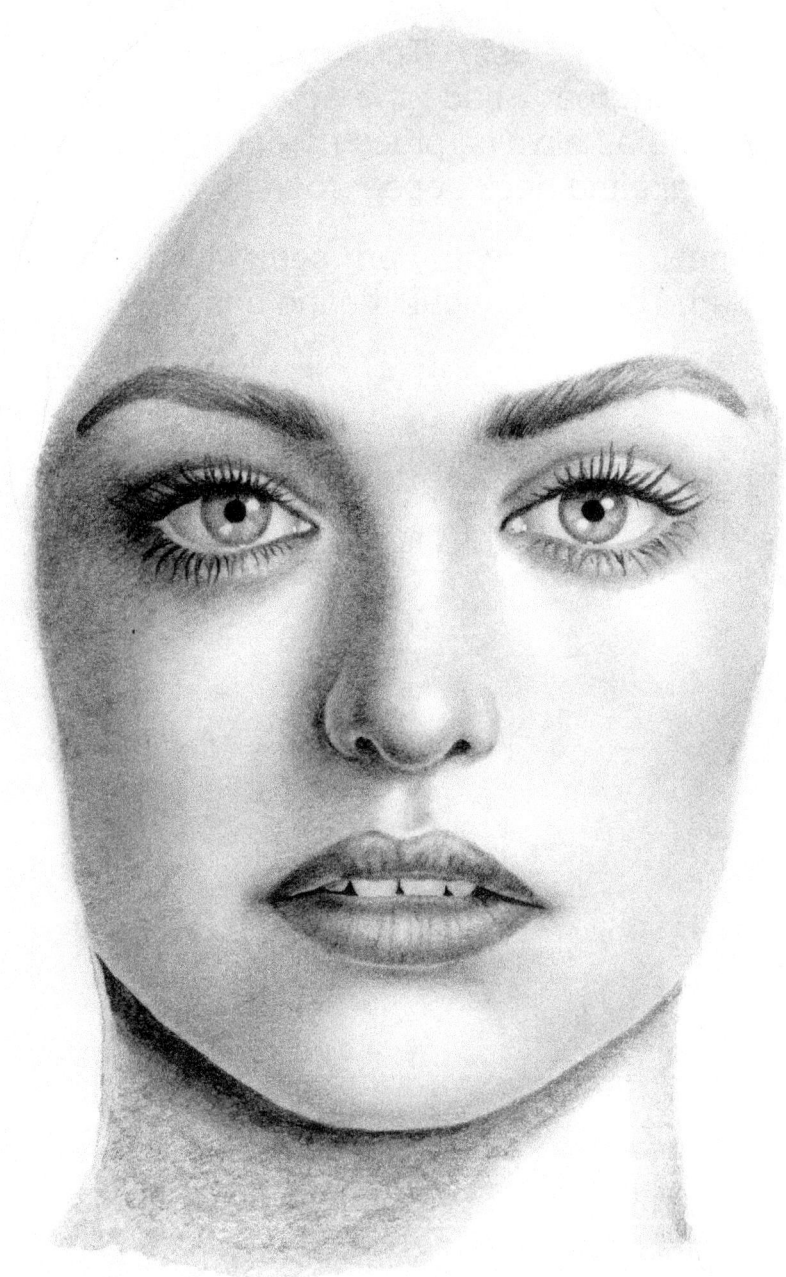

So, finish shading the neck with a 6H and cover the area that is left unshaded. This area also has to be shaded, it shouldn't stay white.

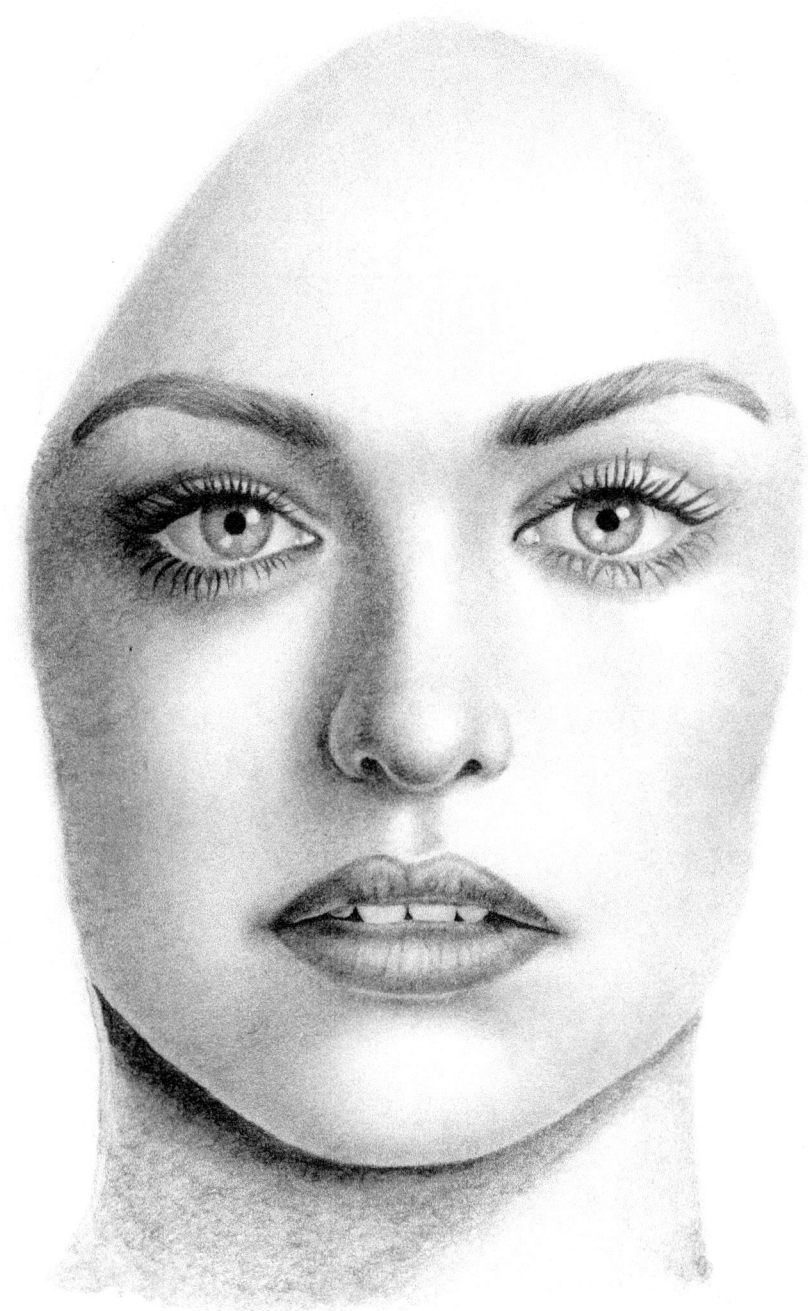

We can blend it all now with a tissue, starting over the
highlights. Press hard to impress the graphite into the
tooth of the paper. Now you can shade more where you

want and blend it again.

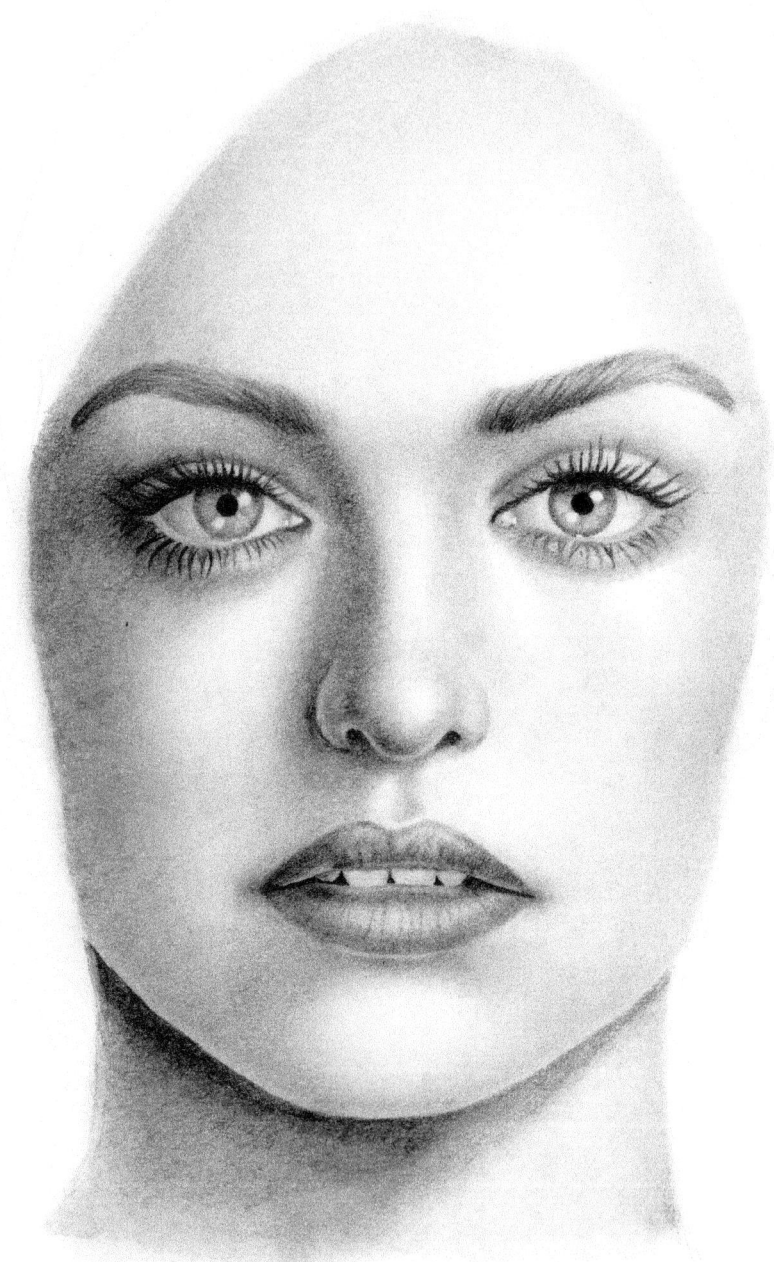

Let me just show you how to shade the ear, in case you'd like to draw it either here or in your future portraits. I start with an HB, marking the darker areas that get less light and cast shadows. You can check up at the reference photos. You shouldn't use darker pencil here. If we draw the left ear, that would be a different story because that side is in a very strong shadow.

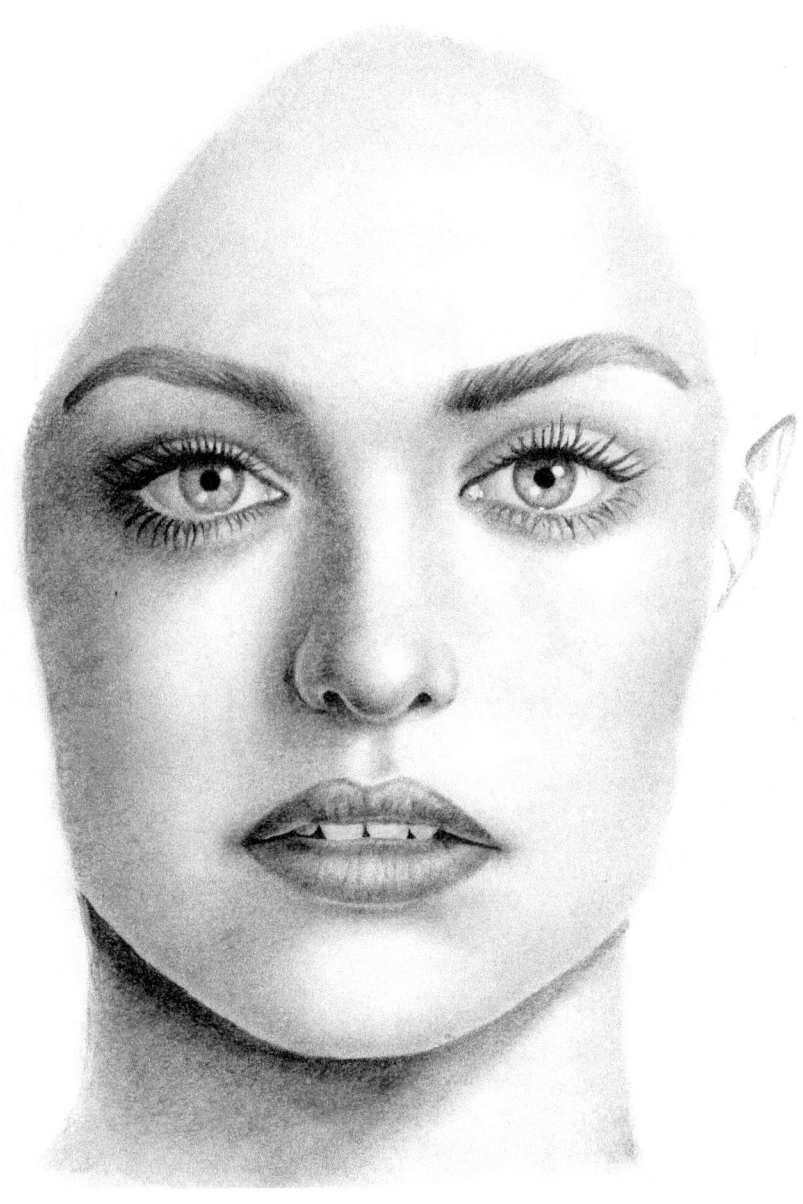

Use a 6H to cover the rest of the ear and mark some highlights with an eraser.

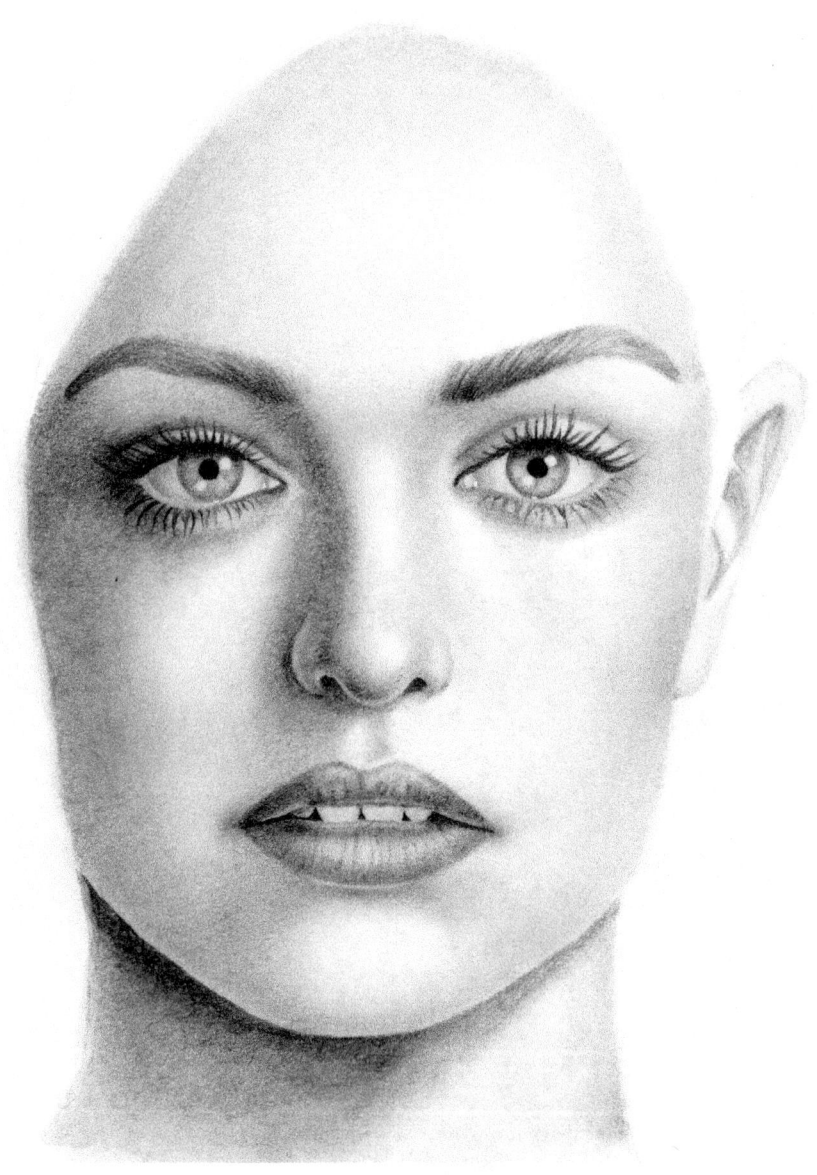

How to Draw Hair

Now we can start drawing the hair.

We have the direction of the hair flow, for example here or in the upper-left part of the head. Take a look at the next image to see how I started and the arrowed lines that you should follow in the next few steps. This way we will get the highlight in midway and the hair will appear shiny. I am using a mechanical pencil with 2B lead in it. So, draw the hairs, one by one, towards the highlight – as shown in the next image. Press harder next to the root of the hair. Apply fast strokes and release the pressure as you approach the highlight. Change the pressure on your pencil and go over some areas multiple times to create a variety of tones.

You can start next to the forehead where the hairs are more straight and make them curvier as you work away from the forehead. Draw much more over the outline of the skull that we created in the very beginning. The outline of the hair should be placed far away from the skull.

Drawing the hair is very time-consuming work and often takes more time than drawing the entire face, so take your time and focus on a small area at once. If you're left-handed, this side may be more difficult to draw, but for right-handed the right side will be more difficult to draw because it is not that handy.

Anyway, you can turn the paper to make it more approachable, but don't forget to lean your hand on a clean piece of paper that you put over your drawing to avoid smudging the drawing. You can go over the forehead as much as you want, you can cover it more or less. Draw some hairs all over the face and over the background randomly.

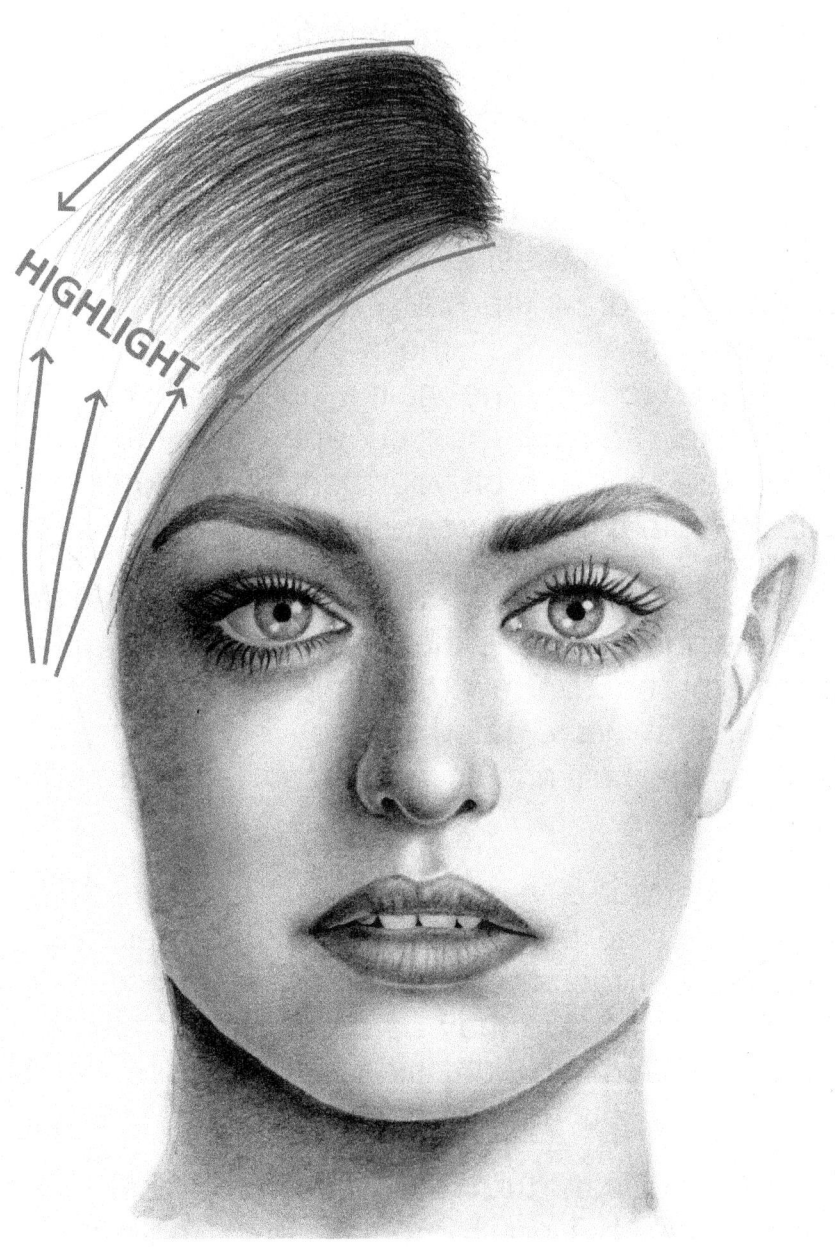

The next thing is to draw from the opposite direction towards the highlights, following the arrowed lines that I placed digitally in the previous image. Still using a 2B lead in a mechanical pencil or a well-sharpened 2B pencil, start at the lower end of the lock, where you want it to be, and draw each hair upwards. As always, press harder over the starting points and release the pressure as you draw towards the highlights.

You can see that this highlight in the middle already gives a shiny effect to the hair. Some of the hairs can go over the highlight.

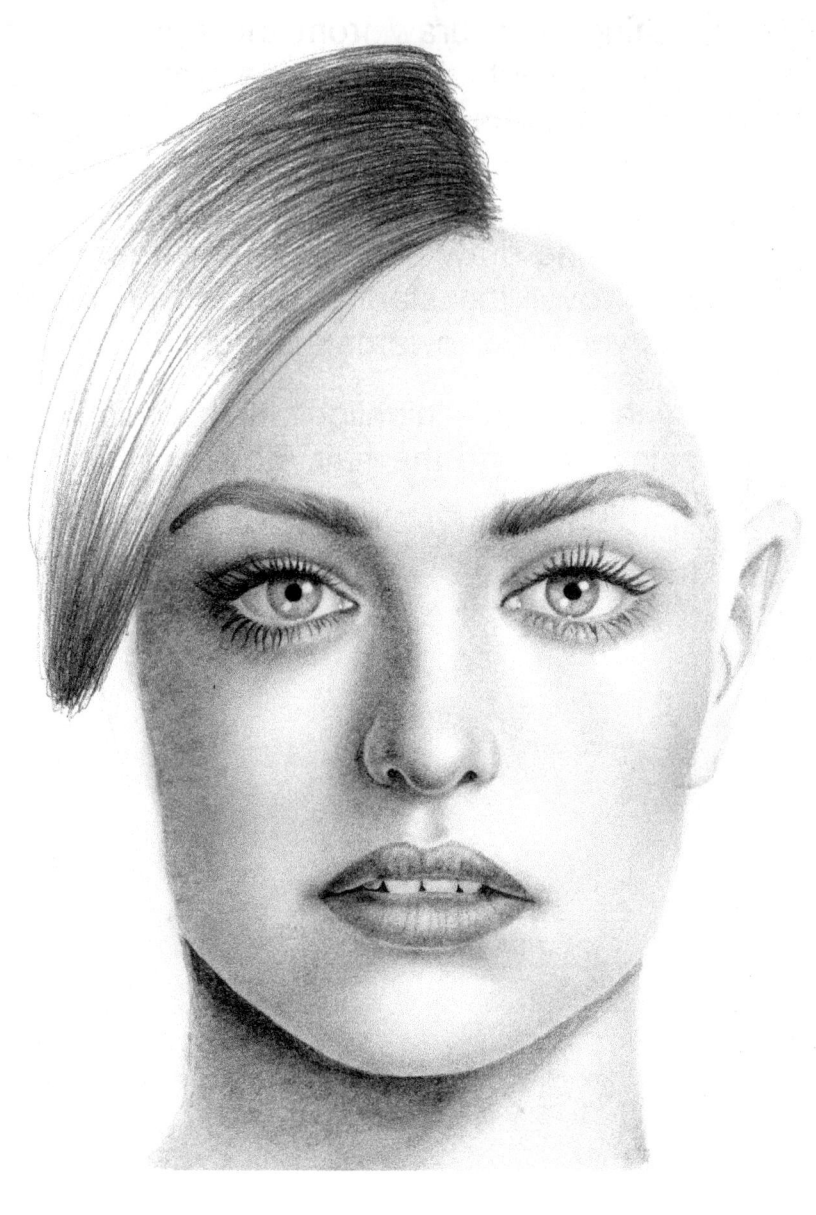

Now you should change your lead to an HB or brighter and continue over this brighter area. If you don't have a mechanical pencil, just use a well-sharpened pencil, and of course, you can choose tones other than what I have. Start over the previously drawn hairs, not on their starting point, but somewhere over them. Do not start over the highlights because there you should already release the pressure and lift off the pencil lead. Don't press too hard because the highlight should stay pretty bright. I want to draw bright brown hair, so the highlights shouldn't be white, but if you draw blonde, the highlights can stay absolute white on some very illuminated areas where the hair bends. Draw from both sides following the direction of those arrowed lines.

Here also, change the pressure to create brighter and darker hairs.

In the next image you can see that I haven't left anything white, the whole area of the highlight is covered with an HB. And also, you can see how the highlight and shadows suggests the roundness of the head.

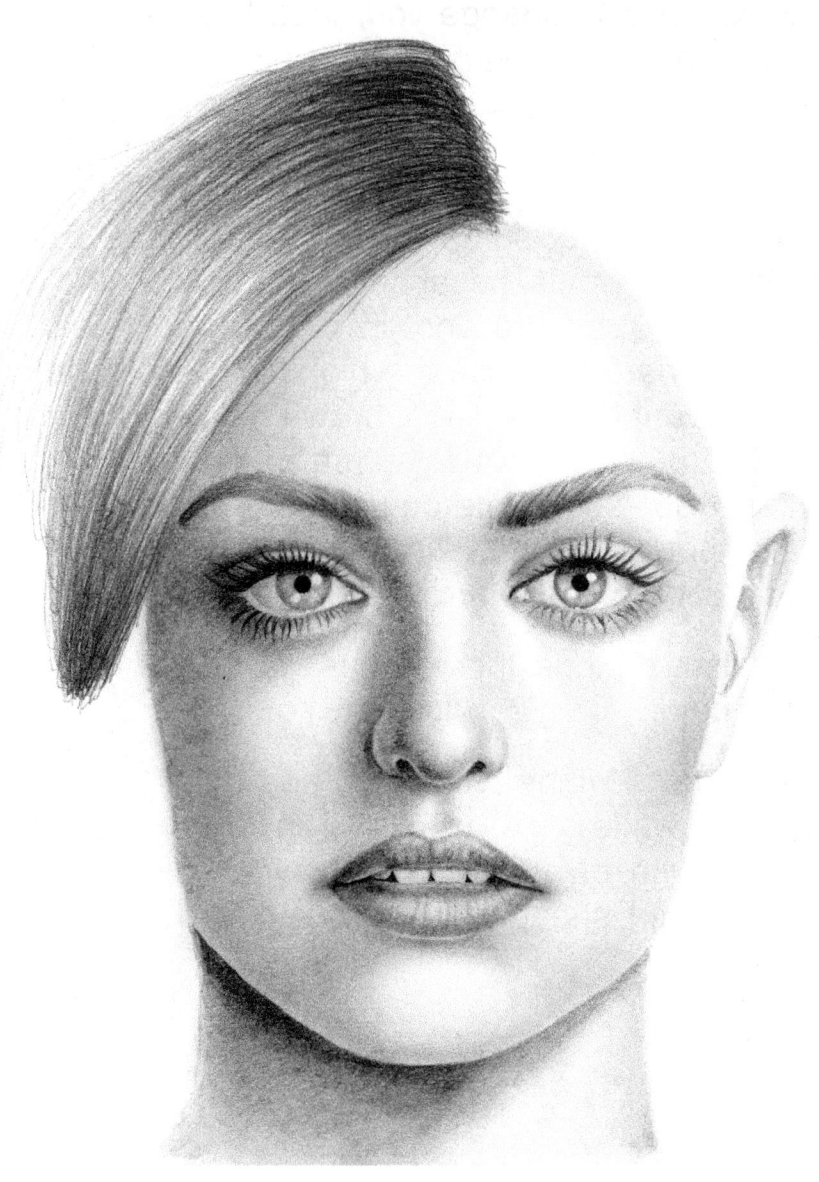

Blend it all with a tissue, starting in the middle, over the brighter areas, and blend towards the darker parts. You shouldn't use circular motions now, but follow those arrived lines, just in the opposite direction, starting over the highlight. Take a new tissue when yours becomes dirty to avoid applying too much graphite over the highlights. In the next image, you can see how the hair appears less harsh, and looks soft.

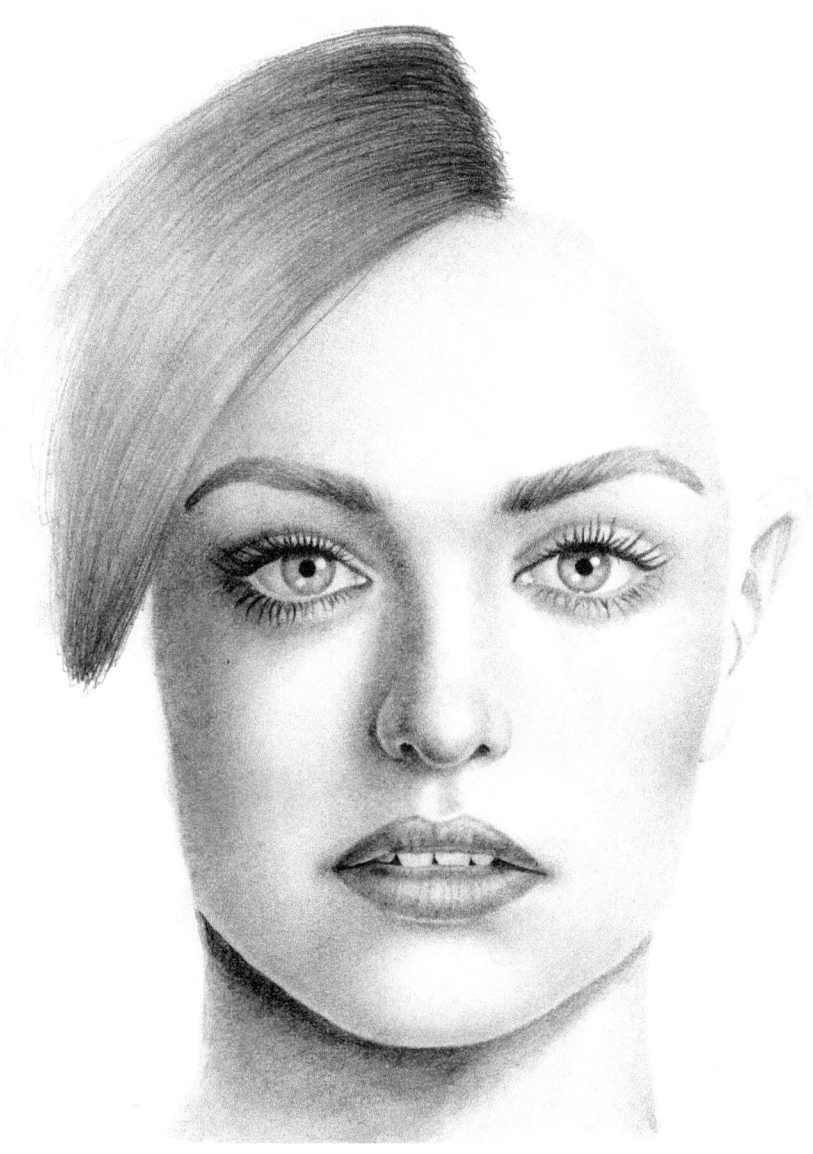

Add some highlighted hairs in the middle and all over the hair, going all over in the unpredictable ways, at random, making quick motions. Use a sharp tip of an eraser and erase out flyaway hairs. Also, press here in the middle of the highlight, and erase the locks towards the darker hair. If you've exaggerated with highlighting, just go over again with a tissue and the highlight will simply disappear.

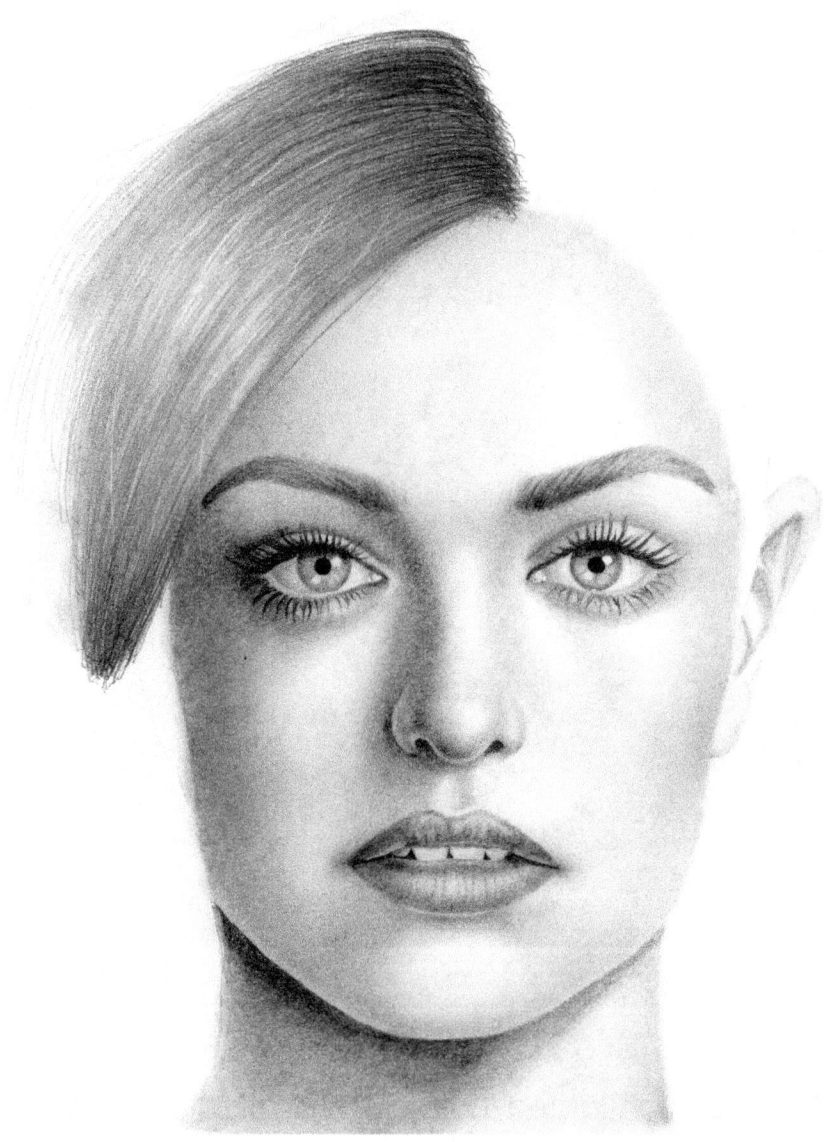

Now we can kind of add more shadows next to the

roots of the hair, using an 8B or any other very dark pencil. Just avoid going over the highlighted hairs that you just created, and make some areas darker with a very dark pencil. Blend it a bit with a blending stump. Don't blend now with a tissue because you can go over the highlights and darken them this way.

Add some darker locks over the highlighted area, using an HB, pressing lightly and blend them with a blending stump. Compare my previous and next image to see the difference and note what I have done in this step.

Also, still using an 8B, draw the hair next to the face under the lock that you drew with a 2B. This way the end of this lock will pop, even though it's pretty dark. Draw next to the face carefully because you're shaping the face. You want to be cautious of messing with the whole shape of the face. Press very lightly first, and if everything looks good, go over that with a 4B or darker pencil. This area should be very dark because it gets no light; even the ear wouldn't be visible, that's why I found it pointless to shade the left ear when I shaded the right ear. If we had more light sources coming from the left side, then there would be a different kind of shading, but I wanted to keep it the technique simple at this time.

Don't cover the whole area on the right side, only draw about .5 of an inch, or 1.5cm next to the face. The rest of the hair, its outer part, has to be drawn with brighter nuance in the following steps, since we want to draw bright brown hair. Draw some quick hairs over the face too to make it look more natural.

Here you have to decide what kind of haircut you want to draw. I want the hair not too long, not too short, but just to draw it as long to cover the paper till the bottom where I have stopped drawing the neck. I want the inner (darker) part of the hair to flow towards the neck. So I'm just drawing the strokes over it with an 8B, but the majority of the hair is behind the neck.

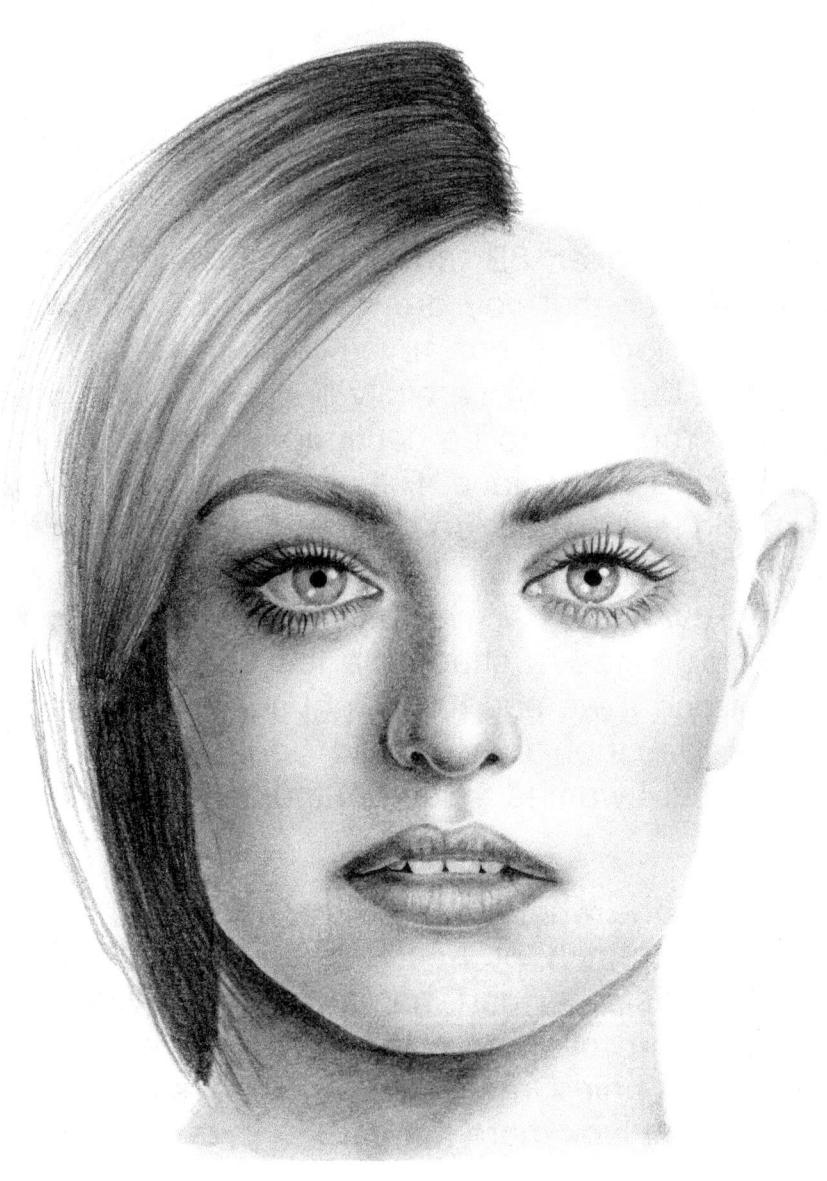

Now we can draw the rest of the hair on the left side, using an HB. We have to use a brighter tone for the outer areas because there the haircut gets more light.

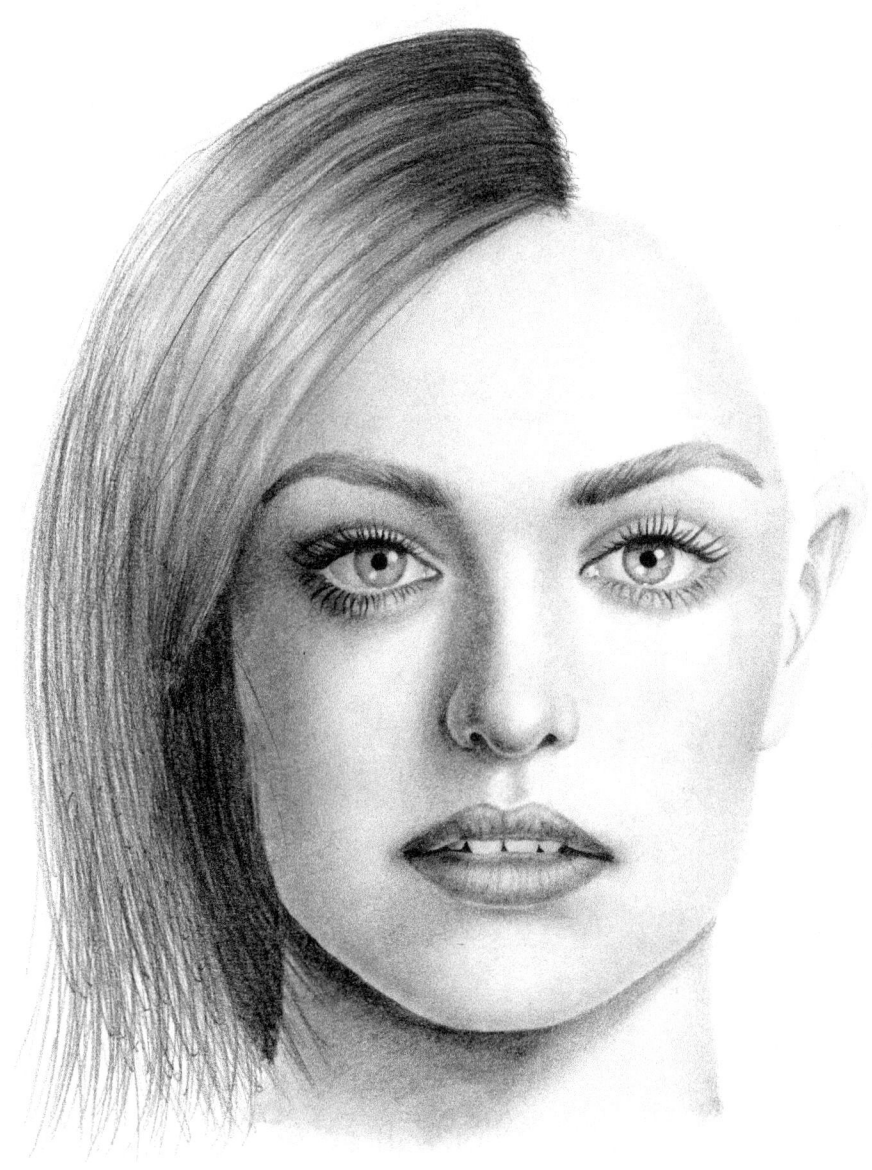

Blend it all, using a tissue.

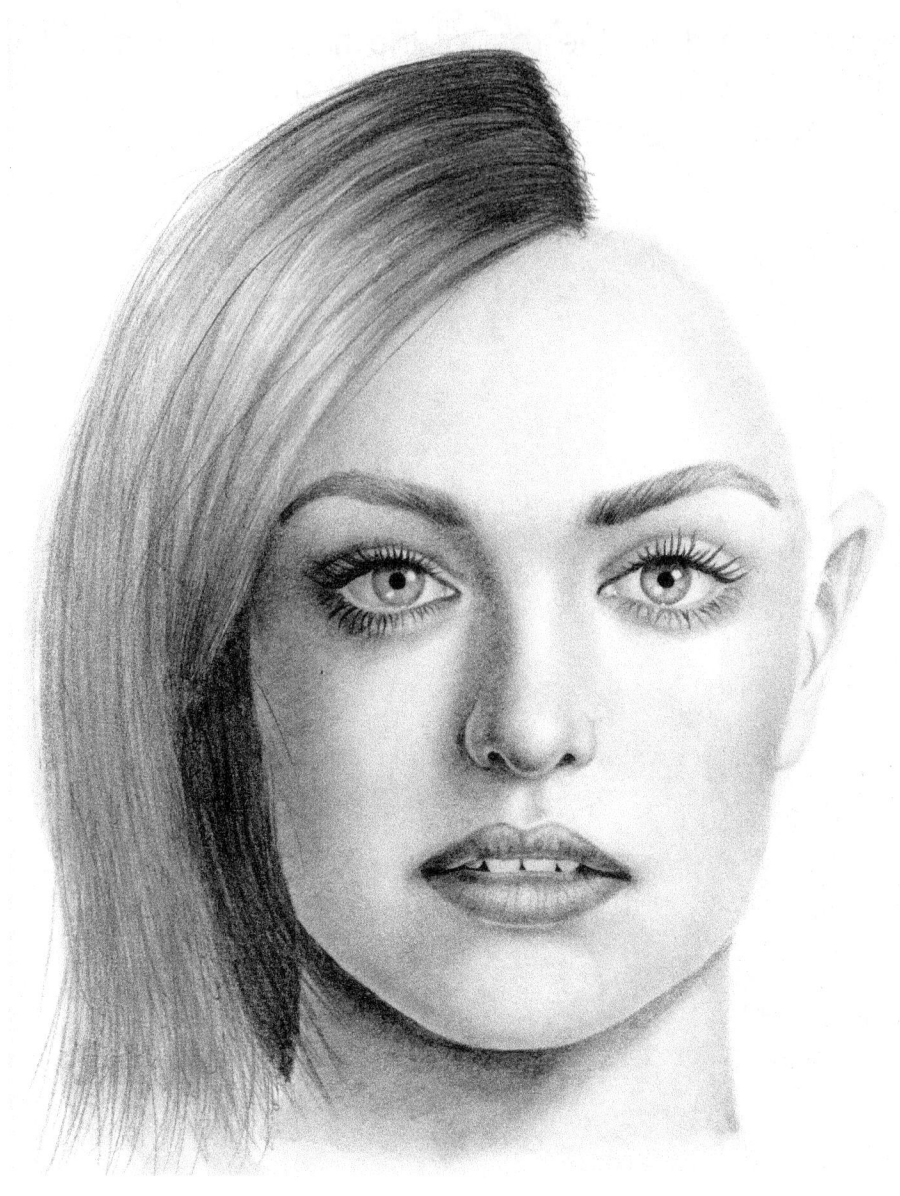

Create the highlighted hairs with an eraser, at random, over the face and the neck too.

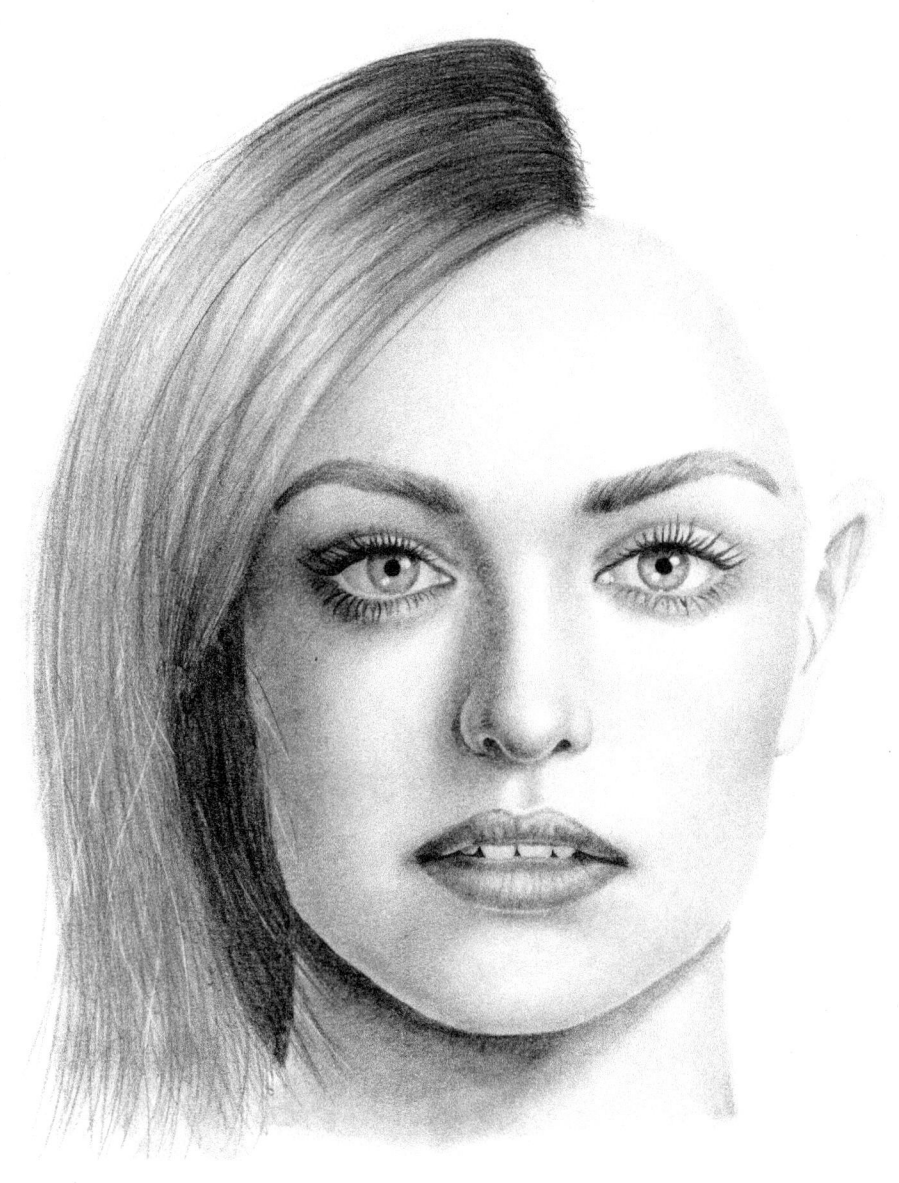

Add some dark hairs over this outer area, using a 4B or darker.

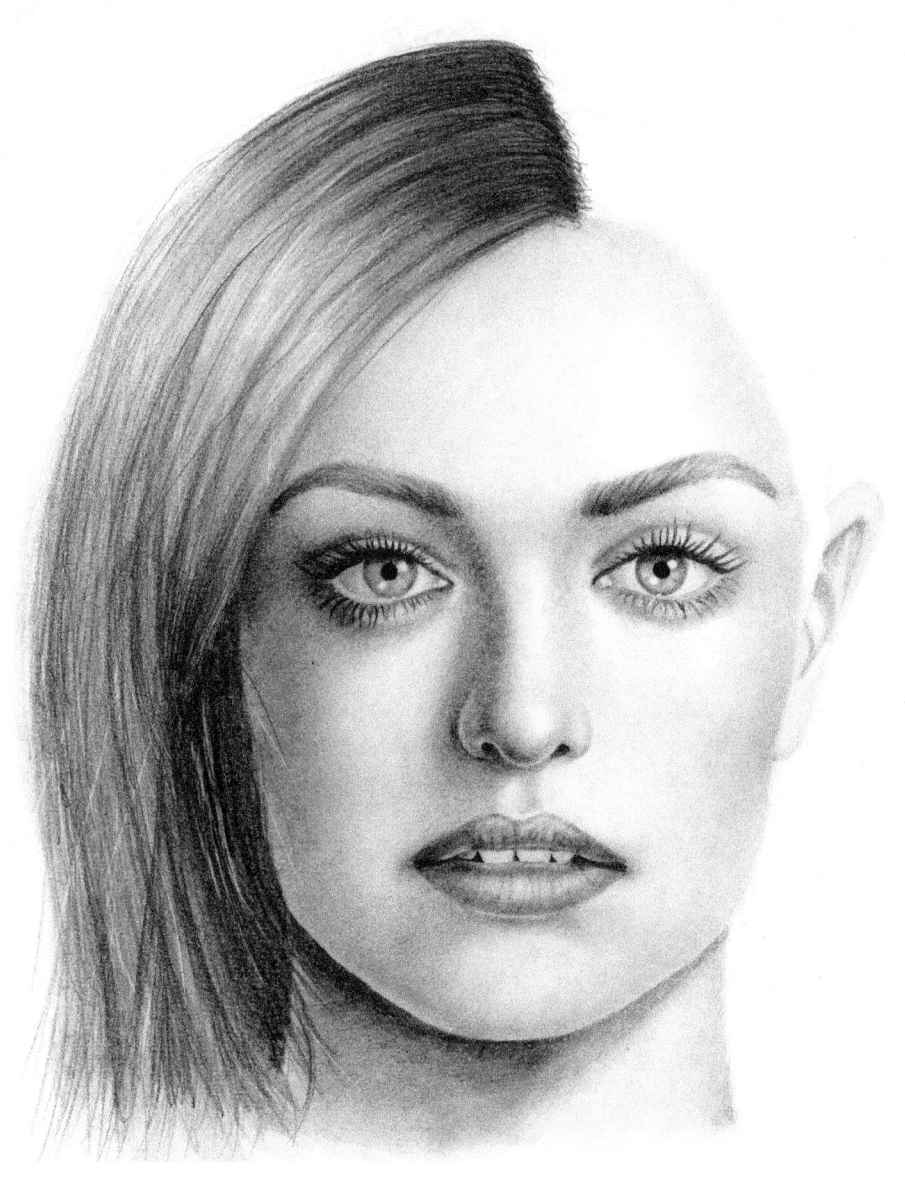

Now, let's move to the right side of the head. Start over the upper-right area and next to the roots of the hair. Leave about 1mm between the areas for the hair division, the visible skin between the two parts of the hair. Using an HB lead in a mechanical pencil, draw the beginning parts of the hairs. Go a bit upwards and then curve it towards the right side. You can see what I mean specifically in the next image.

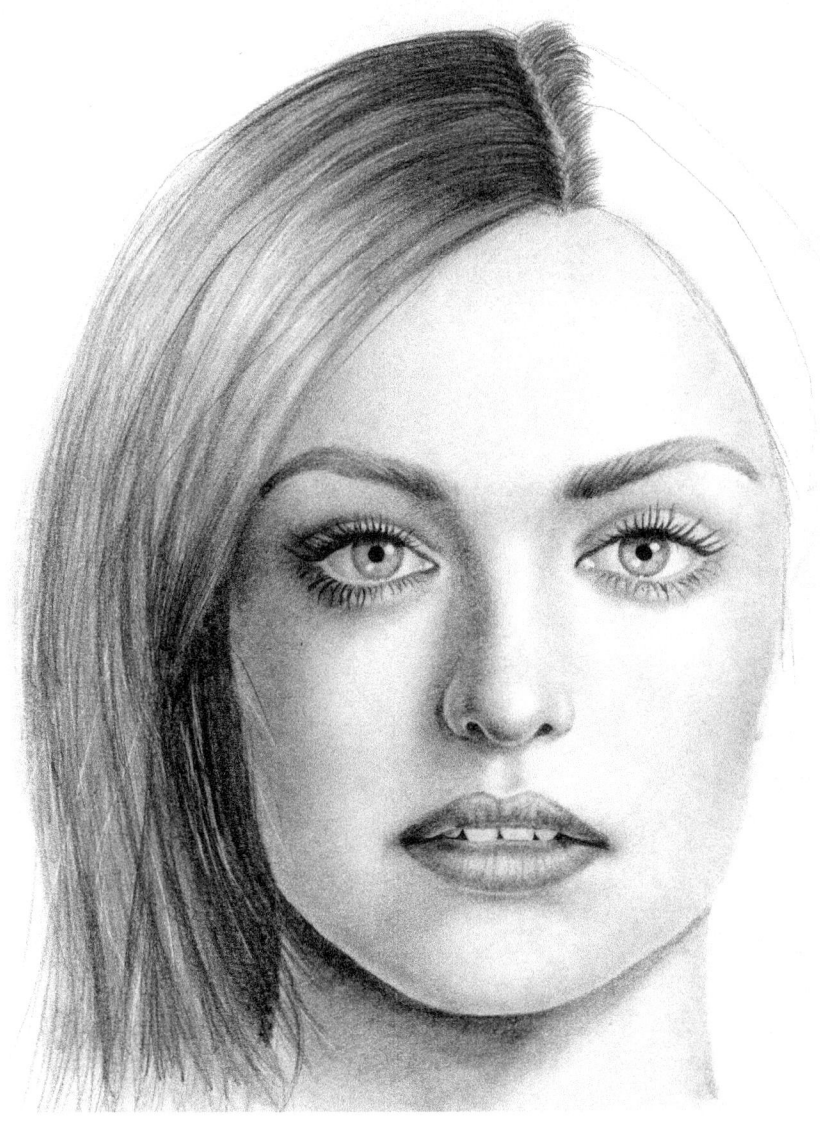

Now use a 2H as a continuation to this area and draw the curvy hairs downwards. We should also create highlights in the upper-right area, as shown in the next picture, so press less as you approach the highlight midway.

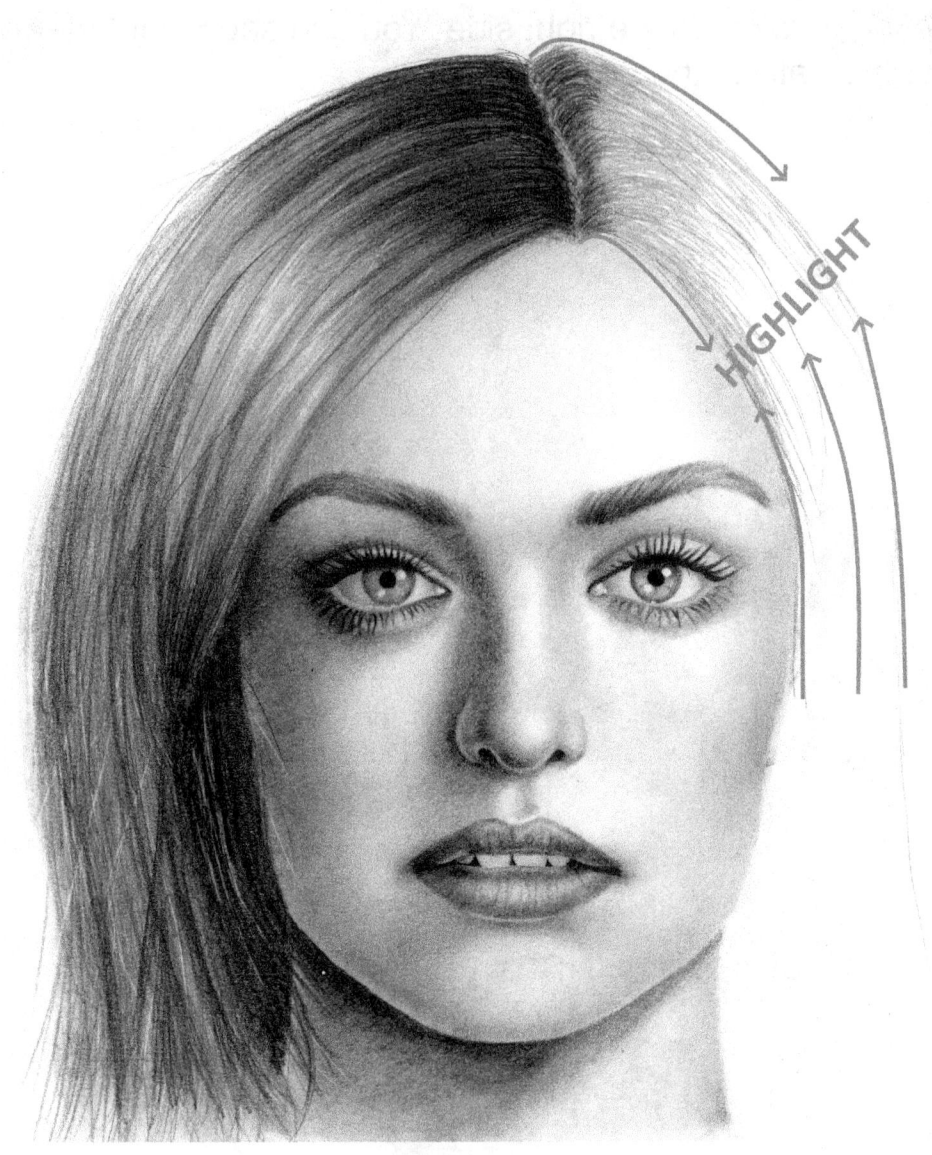

Still using a 2H, follow the arrowed lines from the previous image and draw the hairs towards the highlight. I have deleted my ear because I want to draw the hair over it, but you can see how after drawing and erasing the lines area not showing the same as over the untouched area. This is what I mentioned when I said that once you apply an H or a brighter pencil, the part drawn over that will be always a bit brighter than it would be if you drew it on an untouched piece of paper.

So, start over the ear and draw the lines upwards, towards the highlight, releasing the pressure next to the highlight. For now, the area under the ear is not important because we're going to focus on that area later on.

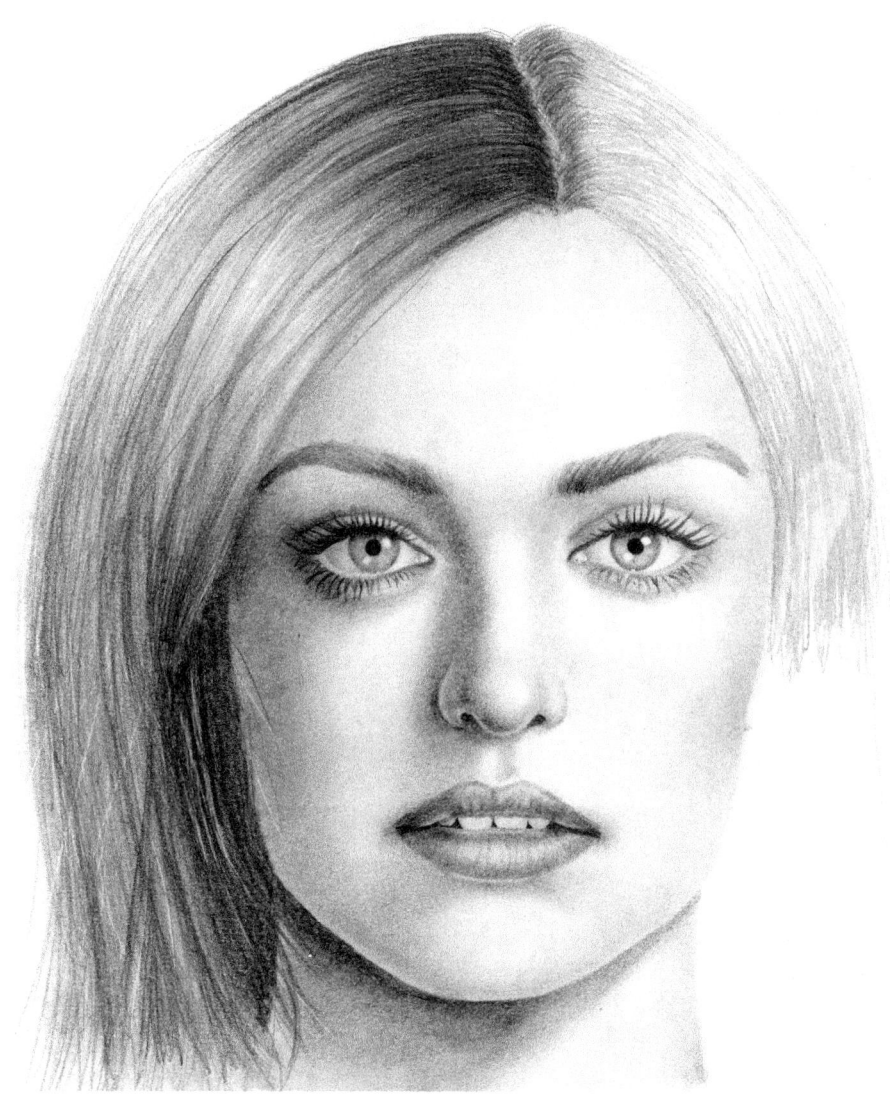

Blend this area with a tissue.

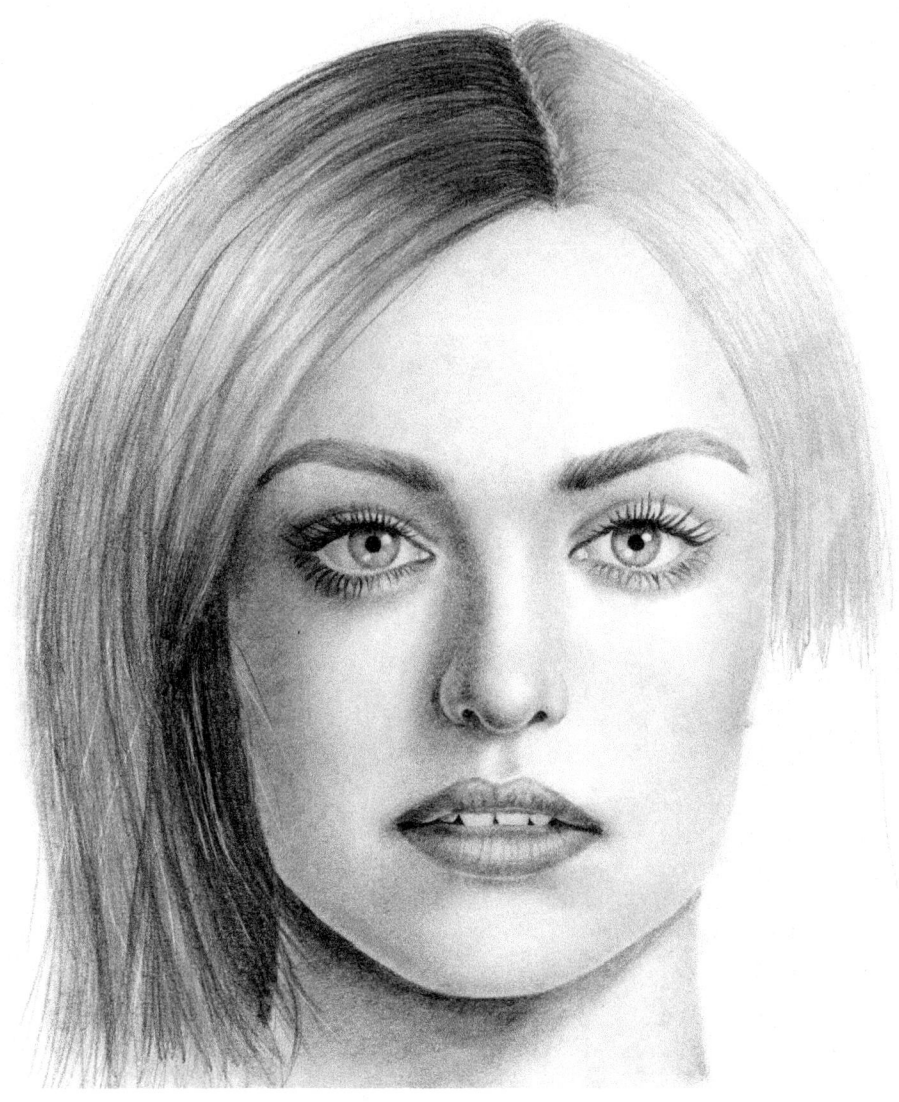

Let's create a darker locks between the hair, or shadowed hair, using an HB. Press a bit harder in the upper area, as a continuation to the ends of the tiny, curvy lines that you drew when you started working on the right side of the hair. Go over the highlights too, pressing gently and always blending everything with a blending stump. To make the visible ear disappear, draw the strokes over the brighter areas pressing harder and press less where the ear isn't visible. If it still stays a bit visible, it is not a big problem because we can often see the ear through the hair. Compare the previous and the next image to see the changes. Note the differences and what have I done in this step.

Create a cast shadow over the forehead and temple, using an HB, pressing lightly and blending it with a clean Q-tip. Add some hairs that fly over the temple and forehead, using quick motions, pressing lightly.

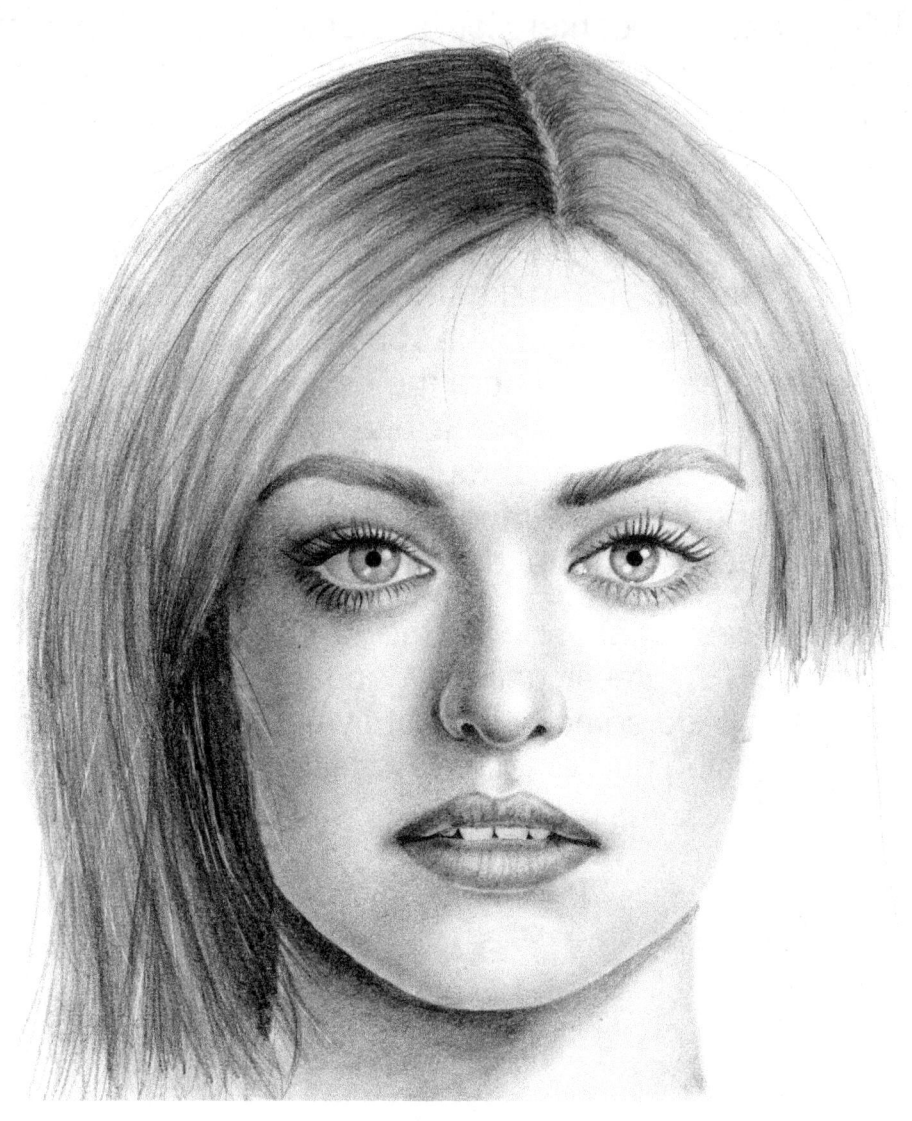

Create some highlighted hairs with the sharp top of an eraser using quick motions. Create more of these over the highlighted area.

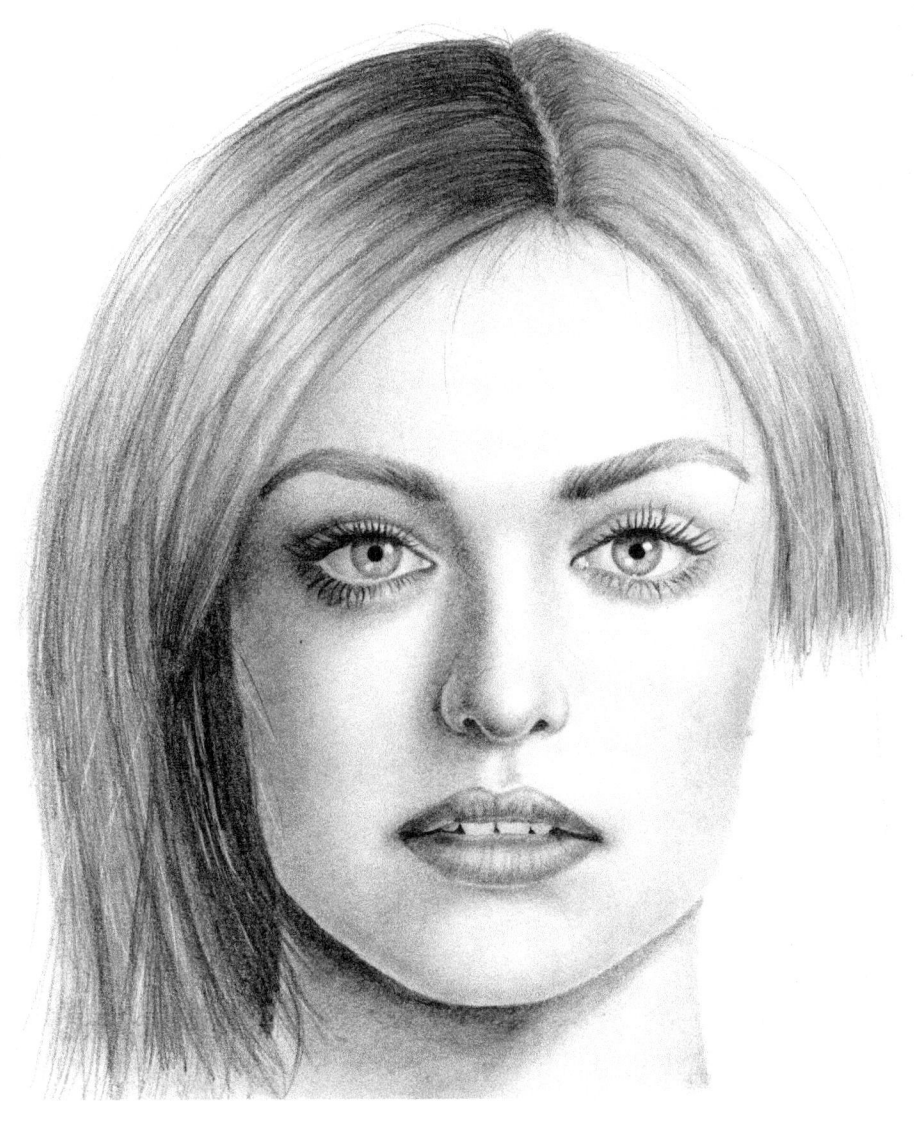

Now we can finish the hair on the right side, under the right ear. Start over the ear and draw the hairs downwards using an HB. The endings can go to the left or to the right, over the neck and the background, at random. The edge between the hair and the background shouldn't be clear because some of the hairs are always flying around.

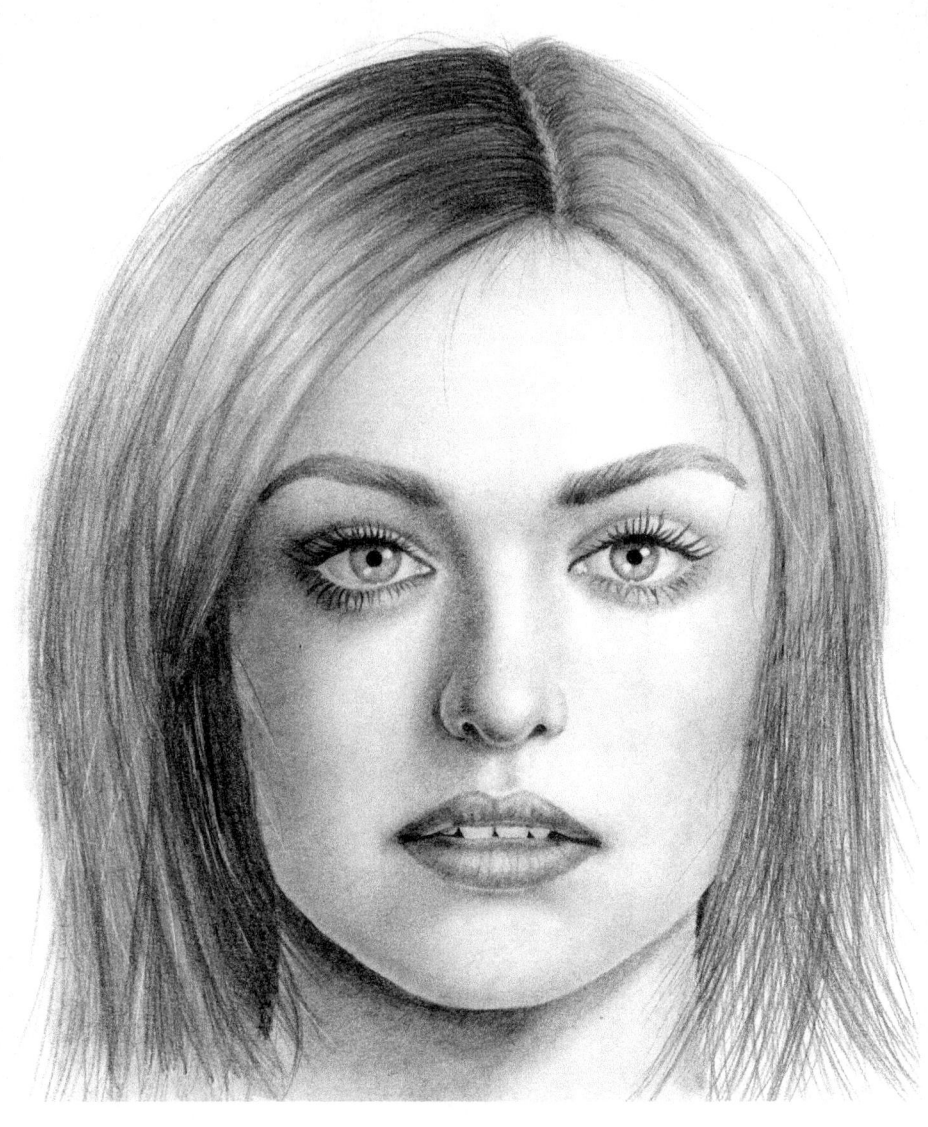

Blend it all with a tissue. You can see in my drawing how after blending, dirty dots have appeared where I accidentally forgot to place the paper under my hand. I will have to shade around these to make them disappear in the last step.

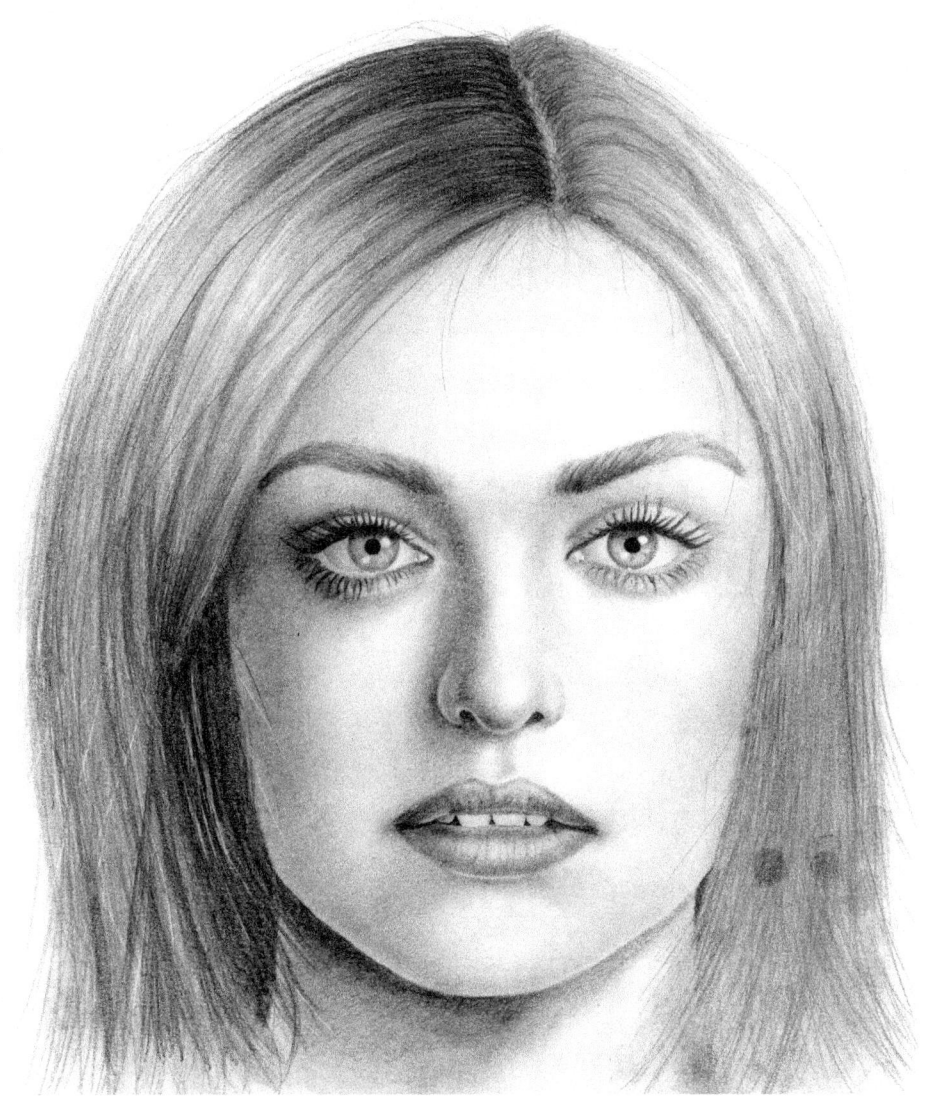

Randomly, add some highlighted hairs all around. As I mentioned before, the randomness is very important. And also, the more tones you created in your drawing, the better.

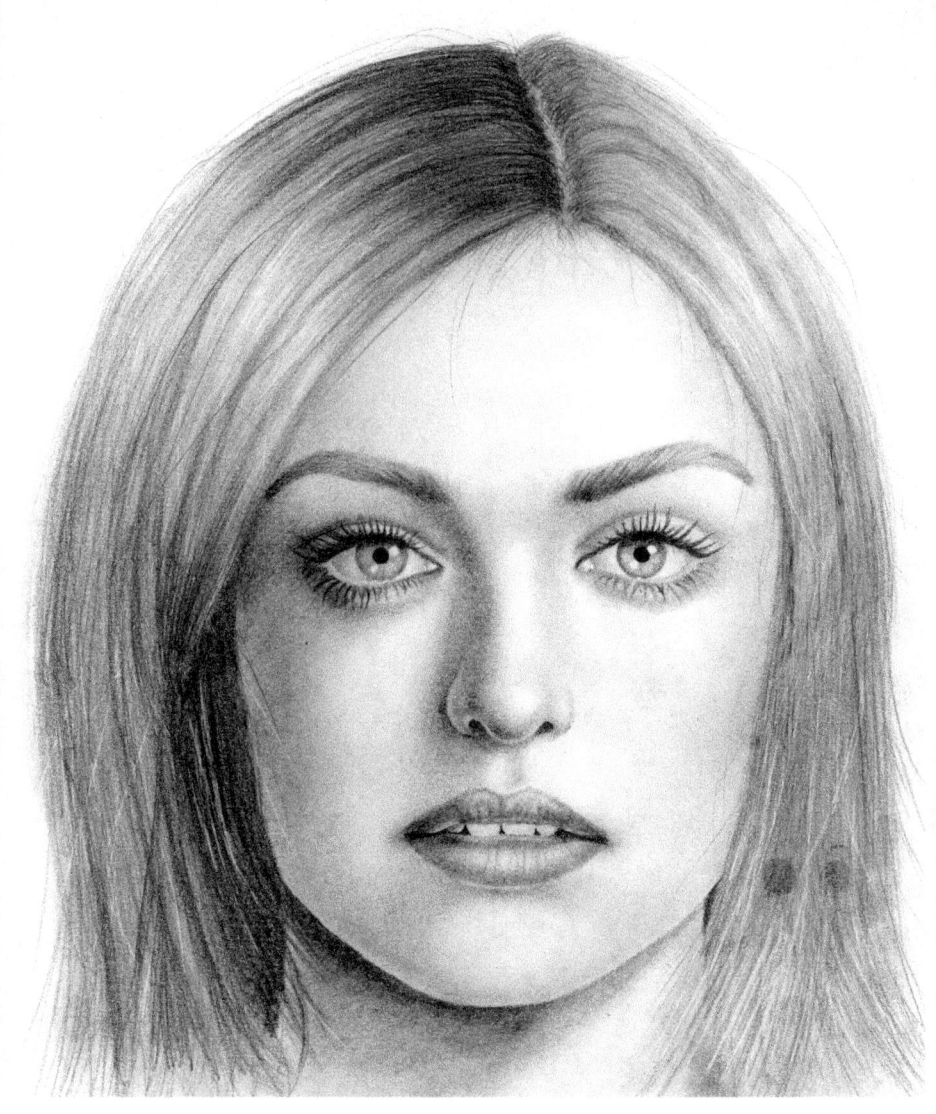

Now we can finish this drawing by adding the shadows inbetween the hair. I also have to shade around the dots to make them disappear. Here, on the right side, we shouldn't create too strong of shadows. Since an HB is pretty dark blend it with a blending stump.

So, this is my portrait from scratch. Any similarity to anyone is a coincidence.

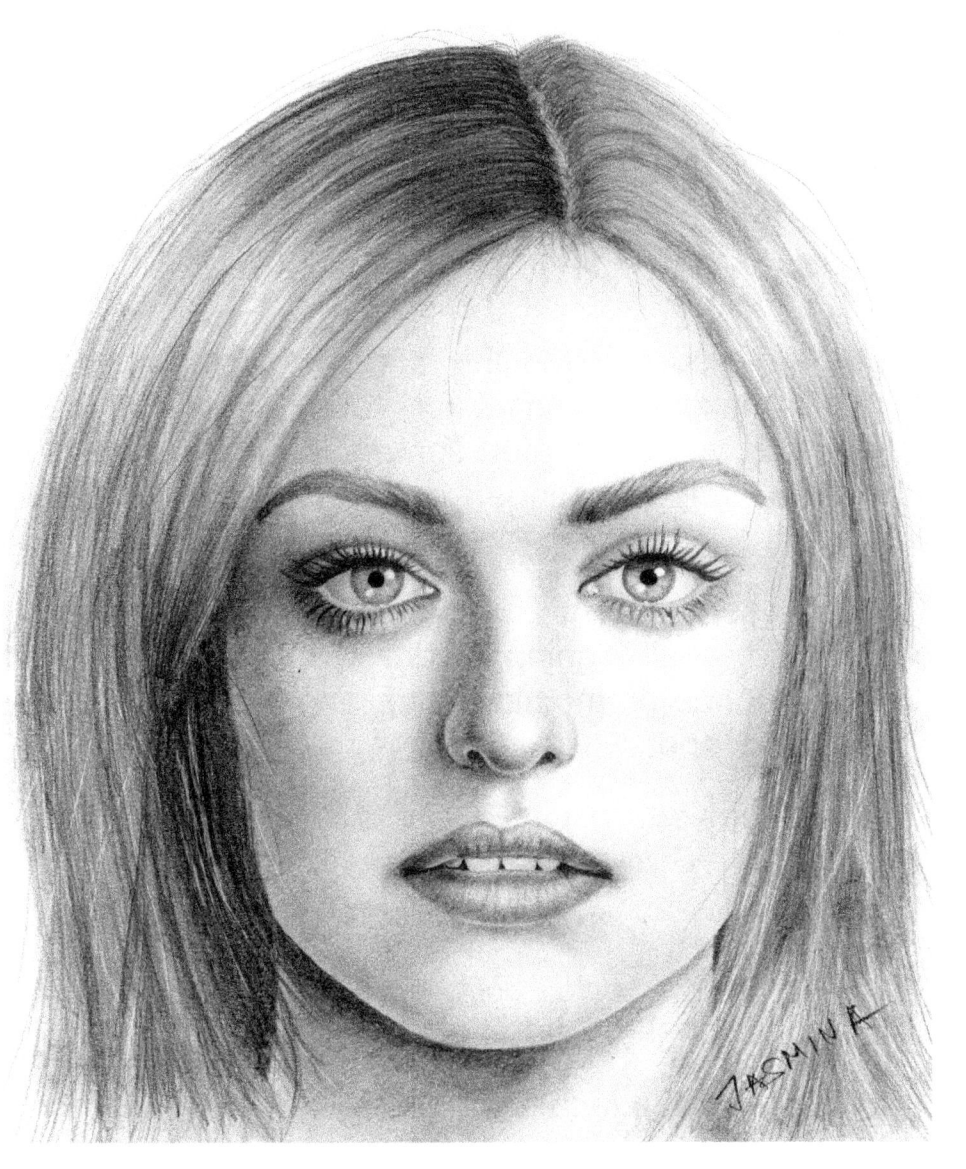

EPILOGUE

I hope that you enjoyed this tutorial and that you can gain the maximum from it for your future portraits. I believe that you've created some satisfying results and that you will continue practicing and working persistently.

You can use this same tutorial for males and for each portrait that you're going to draw. Just make sure to always change something and experiment with the shapes and tones.

I hope to see your results.

A task for you:

Using this tutorial, go step-by-step again, and try to:

- Draw a male face next time.

- Imagine a light source coming from the top, the upper-left corner, the bottom (instead of upper-right corner we used in the tutorial), and shade according to these.

- Draw a wider chin.

- Create straight eyebrows with tiny hairs all around.

- Draw a bigger nose and thinner lips.

- Draw facial hair, mustache, and beard using a 2H over the highlighted skin, an HB over the mid-tone, and a 2B for shadowed parts of the skin.

- Draw on A3 paper format, which is double the size of the one we used in this tutorial, so that you can go much more into detail and to practice. The bigger paper, the more time it will take, thus helping you to cultivate and develop your patience, which is crucial for a realistic style of drawing.

So, try using this tutorial differently. I hope to see your results

About the Author

Jasmina Susak is a self-taught, graphite and colored pencil artist, art teacher and author of more than 17 how-to-draw books. She specializes in creating photorealistic drawings of animals, people, superheroes and everyday objects.

Jasmina graduated and worked as a dressmaker for many years. Now she is a freelance, self-employed artist. It is her full-time job, and she's been doing it professionally since 2011.

Jasmina has hundreds of thousands of followers and subscribers on social media, and her drawing videos have tens of millions of views all around the world.

Jasmina loves animals, science, astronomy, technology, web designing, reading, listening to music. She lives in Hungary, a little country in the middle of Europe.

Visit her website for more tutorials, her drawing gallery, art prints and more.

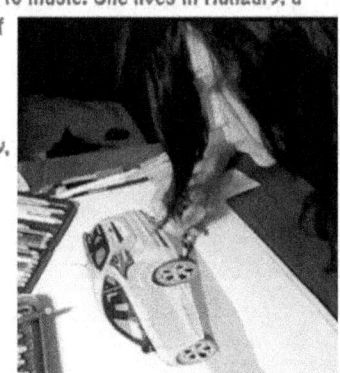

www.jasminasusak.com

If you want to learn faster and better, I recommend joining my website, **Pencil Drawing Tutor**. As a member, you'll learn through real-time narrated videos (even the portrait from this book), step-by-step written tutorials with pictures, and have 24/7 access to **PenPick Graphite**. You can attach your drawings under any tutorial and chat with other members. The lessons are perfect for beginners, those looking to improve, or anyone who wants inspiration and fun.

Brand new tutorial every WEEK.
Come join us!

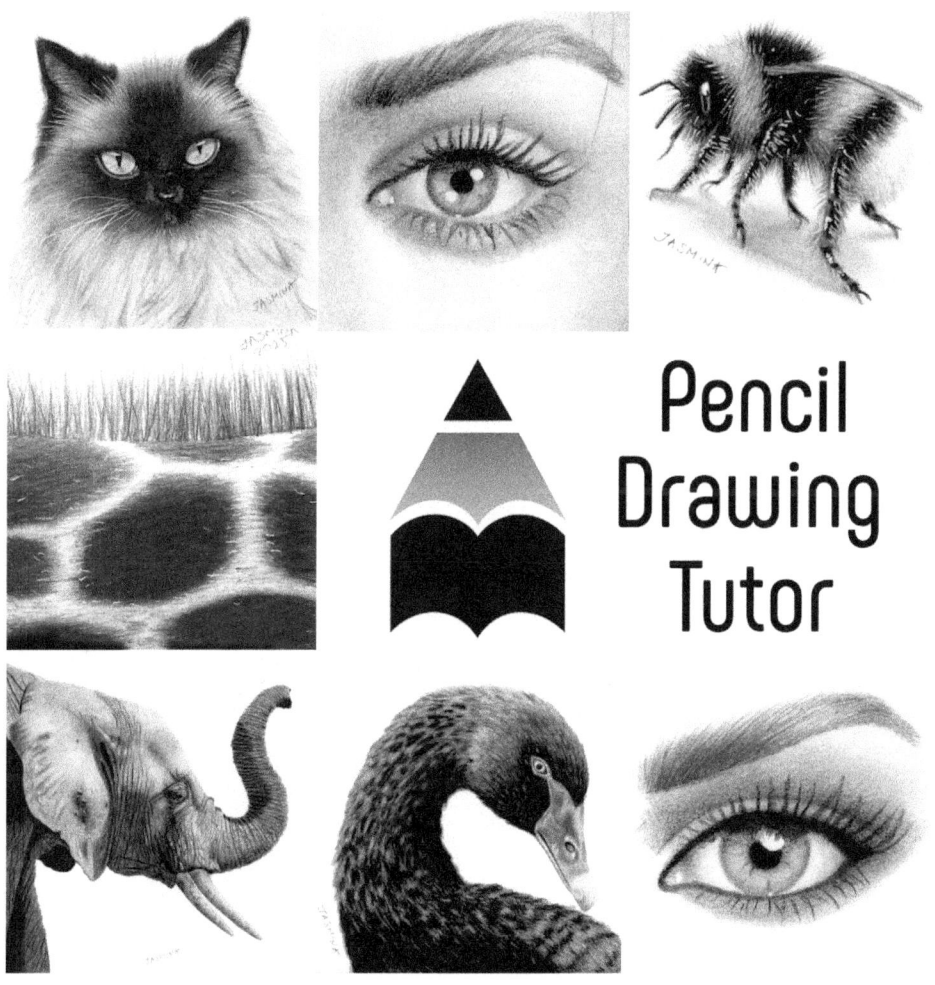

WWW.PENCILDRAWINGTUTOR.COM

www.ingramcontent.com/pod-product-compliance
Lightning Source LLC
Chambersburg PA
CBHW060857170526
45158CB00001B/397